CONTENTS

Section

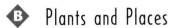

D0884958

How to use this book

This book is more than just a guide to the Gardens. It can be used alongside your free Welcome to Wakehurst leaflet to help you plan your visit and find your way around. But it also shows how the plants in the Gardens reflect our vital international conservation and research work and tells the fascinating history of the estate.

The sections of the book reflect the geographical origins of the plants and the characteristic landscapes of the Weald, showing some of the plants and explaining how our work is leading to a better understanding of such plants and how to protect them. We want you to share in our fascination with the Plant Kingdom and to find out more about what we do as well as what we are.

Use the map and the index on the left if you want to find the sections of the book which deal with particular parts of the Garden that interest you. Throughout the book, the locations where you can see the plants and habitats mentioned are in CAPITAL TYPE.

The Many Faces of Wakehurst Place

The Royal Botanic Gardens at Kew and Wakehurst Place are among the most beautiful gardens in the country. But our beauty is more than skin deep. Our combined living collection of more than 40,000 different kinds of plants is the largest and most diverse in the world – one in eight of all flowering plant species. But it is just one aspect of our world-wide plant research and conservation work. Wakehurst Place, for example, is to be the site of the Millennium Seed Bank, which will conserve seeds from 10 per cent of the world's flowering plants by the year 2010, providing a safety net against the danger of their extinction.

HISTORIC

The Mansion at Wakehurst Place is more than 400 years old but the history of the estate is believed to stretch back even further.

In the surrounding countryside, charcoal deposits and the remains of ironstone mining pits suggest the wooded hills were inhabited by Iron Age peoples.

The name Wakehurst is of Saxon origin and the first owner to have left records was a Norman who is said to have married the daughter of William the Conqueror.

In the 12th century, William de Wakehurst bought the estate from Phillip de Crauele (Crawley) and Wakehursts lived here until the line ended in 1454 with two girls, Margaret and Elizabeth.

THE CULPEPER CONNECTION

Margaret and Elizabeth were made wards of Sir John Culpeper of Bedgebury, a relative of the famous herbalist Nicholas Culpeper. But the girls were abducted by Sir John's brothers, Richard and Nicholas in 1463: 'They appeared with force and arms riotously against the Kynge's peas, arrayed in the maner of warre… the seide Margaret and Elizabeth at the tyme of their takyng away makyng grete pittious lamentacion and wepyng.' But despite the lamentacion and wepying both couples were married very quickly and lived together at Wakehurst, seemingly happily, for another 50 years.

The present mansion was built by Sir Edward Culpeper in 1590, using local sandstone. The last Culpeper to own the estate sold it in 1694 – to pay gambling debts.

1694
Dennis Lydell buys Wakehurst from the last Culpeper

1757
The Clarke family inherit the Wakehurst estate

1776
The estate passes to the Peytons, a distinguished naval family

1869
Dowager Marchioness of Downshire buys Wakehurst

WAKEHURST ◆A

DEVELOPING WAKEHURST'S GARDENS

We have no records about what the gardens, if any, were like in Elizabethan times.

There were rhododendrons and exotic trees in Westwood Valley by the time the Marchioness of Downshire bought Wakehurst but it was Gerald Loder (top), a passionate plantsman, who set the pattern for the development of Wakehurst into one of the country's most beautiful gardens. He subscribed to many of the plant collecting expeditions that were bringing back new and exotic species, especially from eastern Asia, home of some of the world's most beautiful plants. He also built up an outstanding collection of species from South America, Australia and New Zealand.

Sir Henry Price (bottom) continued developing the gardens and the work of these men forms the backdrop to today's scientific collections, established and maintained by the Royal Botanic Gardens, Kew. Wakehurst is now a modern and internationally important botanic garden.

1890	1903	1936	1963
She sells to Sir William Boord MP, who carried out much renovation and restoration	Boord sells to Gerald Loder, later Lord Wakehurst	Loder dies, Wakehurst bought by Sir Henry Price	Wakehurst bequeathed to National Trust, who lease it to Royal Botanic Gardens, Kew

PLANTS & PLACES

B

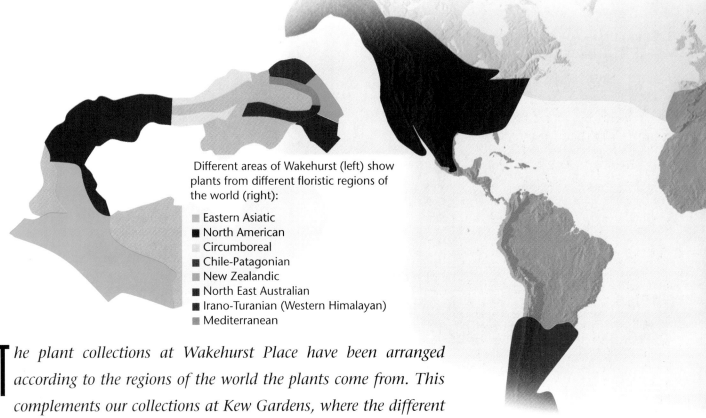

Different areas of Wakehurst (left) show plants from different floristic regions of the world (right):

- Eastern Asiatic
- North American
- Circumboreal
- Chile-Patagonian
- New Zealandic
- North East Australian
- Irano-Turanian (Western Himalayan)
- Mediterranean

The plant collections at Wakehurst Place have been arranged according to the regions of the world the plants come from. This complements our collections at Kew Gardens, where the different types of plants are arranged to show the evolutionary relationships between them.

If you show botanists in South America a photograph of Wakehurst's native and semi-natural woodlands in Spring, they will instantly recognise it as being somewhere in north-western Europe because of the unique combination of beech and oak woods with bluebells, which occurs nowhere else. Plant geographers, ignoring political boundaries, have divided the world into six major areas – called kingdoms – based on their unique assemblies of plant families. Each kingdom contains several regions, based on its genera and species; and each region has a number of provinces with its own unique combinations of species.

At Wakehurst, some of the most important floristic areas of the world's temperate regions are represented by some of their characteristic plants. The collections concentrate on North America, Europe and Asia, South America and Australasia.

OUR PLACE

The largest of all the Kingdoms is called the Holarctic and covers all of Europe, some of northern Africa, non-tropical Asia and most of North America. The Holarctic is made up of nine Regions. The Circumboreal Region is the world's largest and stretches right around the globe. The British Isles is in its Atlantic-European Province.

ARMEN TAKHTAJAN

One of Russia's foremost botanists, Armen Takhtajan is a champion of the idea of classifying the world's vegetation into distinctive areas, each with its characteristic assemblies of plants.

His ideas stemmed from his research into the origins of flowering plants and how the different groups of plants evolved as they migrated around the world.

He believes that understanding these phytogeographic regions can help concentrate conservation work on areas with the greatest diversity of unique plants. He visited Wakehurst in 1992, during our celebrations to mark the end of the work of clearing the damage from the 1987 storm. Many of our new plantings follow his ideas on plant geography.

HOW PLANTS SPREAD ROUND THE WORLD

When flowering plants first appeared, around 100 million years ago, Africa, India, South America, Australia and Antarctica were all part of one huge super-continent – Gondwana. Europe, Asia and North America were also joined, as Laurasia. Flowering plants first appeared in Africa but new types quickly evolved and spread into other continents before they split apart. Later, in other places, continents collided, throwing up mountains that stopped further movement of some types of plants.

The distribution of plants around the world today reflects their evolution in relation to the movement of the continents and to climate change. For example, the spectacular proteas (far left) of the South African Cape and the banksias (left) of Australia are members of the same plant family (Proteaceae).

The family must have first appeared when the continents were joined but these genera have since evolved separately as the continents drifted apart and their environments changed.

The world at the dawn of flowering plants

ASIA AND AMERICA

The tulip tree (*Liriodendron tulipifera*) from the eastern parts of North America, is very similar to the Chinese *Liriodendron chinense* but there are no tulip trees anywhere in between. Botanists believe liriodendrons evolved on land between Alaska and North-East Asia when the continents were closer and their climates warmer than now. As the continents drifted north and the climates cooled plants were forced to migrate south, one branch ending up as *L. tulipifera* in America, the other as *L. chinense* in Asia. Many other groups of plants are also found in both continents but nearly always they are more diverse in Asia. For example there are about 50 species of maple in North America but more than 100 in Asia (and only a dozen or so native to Europe).

TONY SCHILLING ASIAN HEATH GARDEN

Up in the mountains the climate is too harsh for trees. Here you find heathlands with a characteristic vegetation of plants adapted to withstand extremes of rain, temperature and wind. Dwarf rhododendrons are the most important plants – the equivalent of heathers on British moorlands. Alongside the rhododendrons grow shrubs such as cotoneaster, potentilla, gaultheria and juniper and occasionally small trees. This kind of vegetation is common on the mountains right across Asia, represented at Wakehurst by the TONY SCHILLING ASIAN HEATH GARDEN.

The Garden is divided into beds to show species from different mountain regions of Asia: Korea, Sino-Himalayas, Taiwan and Japan.

EASTERN HIMALAYAS

The Eastern Himalayas is one of the world's richest temperate regions for plants, with some 4,000 species, many of which have become garden favourites. Below the tree line are beautiful semi-evergreen forests of rhododendrons, laurels, maples, alders, oaks, birch and conifers. In the WESTWOOD VALLEY *at Wakehurst we are rebuilding our collections, particularly of rhododendrons, to give a taste of this kind of environment. The rhododendron collection will eventually show how these plants vary across Asia. The nearby* HIMALAYAN GLADE *shows how the vegetation might look 3,000 metres up into the mountains, where secondary woodland of berberis, cotoneaster, rhododendron, birches and firs grows up after forest has been cleared for grazing.*

ASIA ◆

Plants from the temperate regions of Asia hold a special fascination for gardeners and botanists alike. In whatever genus of garden plants you care to name the choicest species almost always come from Asia – the most beautiful flowers, the most attractive bark, the fieriest autumn colours.

Eastern Asia in particular is an important region for botanists studying the relationships between the plants of the whole of the Northern Hemisphere. It was one of the major centres of evolution of flowering plants and conifers, and species that can be recognised as fossils millions of years old – such as ginkgos and dawn redwoods – still survive.

This huge diversity is a result of the geological history of the region. Ice ages forced plants to migrate across the only place on Earth with an unbroken landmass stretching from tropics to tundra and there is a tremendous diversity of habitats from high mountains to lush valleys.

HIMALAYAN BLUE POPPY

A single dried specimen of Meconopsis betonicifolia *was sent to Europe from China in 1886 but it was not until 1924 that Frank Kingdon-Ward sent the first seeds from the India-Tibet border so that the plant could be grown in Britain. There are many species of Meconopsis with red, blue, purple, orange and white flowers and all but one originates in Asia – mostly China and the Himalayas. The exception is M. cambrica, the Welsh poppy, a native of western Europe.*

Plant families separated by vast tracts of ocean

SOUTHERN HEMISPHERE

The Earth's Northern Hemisphere is dominated by the continents of Europe, Asia and North America which stretch around the globe and plants have been able to spread relatively freely by land. By contrast in the Southern Hemisphere, the land-masses of South America, southern Africa and Australia and New Zealand are separated by vast tracts of ocean. Temperate plants growing on these continents have less freedom of movement around the globe because they are rarely transported across vast distances of ocean by birds or on ocean currents.

That is why one of the most enduring puzzles in the study of plants was the distribution of related plant species in the Southern Hemisphere. For example, forests of southern beech (Nothofagus species) are found in places as far apart as South America, New Zealand and parts of Australia. Even the same species can turn up on different continents. For example, Hebe elliptica is found in both New Zealand and Patagonia, South America. We now know this was a result of the way continents have moved around on the Earth's surface by continental drift.

NEW ZEALAND

New Zealand has a flora quite unlike anywhere else. The land that eventually became New Zealand was isolated before many flowering plant groups had evolved. Ferns, however, were already widespread and tree ferns are particularly characteristic of New Zealand. In other places they were replaced by conifers and flowering trees.

Hebes were one of the flowering plant groups that managed to spread to New Zealand before it became too isolated and have evolved to fill many ecological roles, from small shrubs to woodland trees.

SOUTHERN BEECHES

Southern beeches (*Nothofagus* species) are related to our own beech trees and are the dominant trees in the temperate woodlands of the Southern Hemisphere. They are found in South America, Australia and New Zealand.

Nothofagus woodland is the natural vegetation of the western side of South America from just below the tropics to the extreme southern tip. They form dense evergreen forests in the north, and more open deciduous woodlands in the south where southern beeches mix with larches and monkey puzzles. These temperate forests are as much under threat from logging as the highly publicised rainforests further north.

Wakehurst Place holds the National Collection of *Nothofagus* with some 17 species currently growing in the estate. We have recently been collecting extensively throughout the natural range of these trees so that the collections represent the natural variation of each species. The *Nothofagus* plantings in COATES' WOOD are only very young but the trees have been planted very close so that eventually you will have a good impression of Southern Hemisphere temperate rainforest. The trees will also help provide windbreak protection for this part of the Gardens.

The Collection is an important reference for botanists as well as helping to conserve this important group of plants whose natural habitats are threatened.

At Wakehurst we are building up our collections of some elements of the temperate flora of the Southern Hemisphere (for example, hebes, left), particularly in the SOUTHERN HEMISPHERE GARDEN *near the* MANSION *and in* COATES' WOOD. *The spectacular flora of the African Cape and Australia are well represented in the Temperate Collections at* KEW GARDENS.

AMERICAN DREAM

◆E

T he first Europeans to land in America found a seemingly endless blanket of primeval forest. In the east, deciduous woodlands of oak, hickory and maple; in the north and west vast tracts of coniferous forest. Although the native Americans had made little demand on the forests for thousands of years the new arrivals soon began wholesale clearance of forests to provide timber and land for agriculture. Today little of the old growth forest remains.

Botanists divide the North American forests into seven distinctive provinces based on their climate and the trees they contain. All but one, the sub-tropical West-Indian Province, are represented in **HORSEBRIDGE WOOD**.

APPALACHIAN

Eastern deciduous broadleaf forest is famous for its autumn colour. Here is found the widest variety of species in North America: oak, hickory, maple and beech with conifers at higher altitudes and in the north.

Virginia round-leaf birch (*Betula uber*) was discovered in 1914 but was later presumed extinct. Fifteen trees were found in 1975 and it is now regarded as endangered.

BIRCH BARK CANOE

Native American canoes were skinned with sheets of the easily peeled, waterproof bark of paper birch, sewn together with roots of white pine and sealed with resin from the same tree.

GULF & SOUTH COAST

Extensive pine forest is the characteristic vegetation on poor soils, with frequent forest fires. Broadleaved trees grow in lower, wetter areas or higher areas away from fire danger.

Swamp cypress (*Taxodium distichum*) is one of only a few conifers that are deciduous. It grows on floodplains and muddy river banks.

VANCOUVERIAN

Along the Pacific coast, from central California up into Alaska – where a continuous belt of coniferous forest thrives – warm ocean currents ensure mild winters and humid air, with plenty of rain and frequent mists and fog. Here grow the tallest and most massive trees in the world: the redwoods, Douglas fir, sitka spruce and western hemlock.

The coast redwood (*Sequoia sempervirens*) is the world's tallest tree (maximum 115 metres and up to 4·6 metres wide). They grow in a narrow coastal belt from California to Oregon. The average age of mature trees is 500 years but they can live for 2,000 years or more.

CALIFORNIAN

Climate of mild winters and hot dry summers, similar to the Mediterranean region. Many of the plants found here grow nowhere else in North America and are often restricted to very small areas, for example Monterey pine and cypress on the narrow coastal fringe between the mountains and the sea.

Monterey pine (*Pinus radiata*) is rare in the wild and found in natural stands in only three places but is one of the world's most commonly planted forestry species.

WEST-INDIAN

Sub-tropical vegetation of the flat lands of southern Florida and the Caribbean Islands. Mangroves dominate the coasts, with palms, persimmons and evergreen oaks inland. Such plants are not frost hardy and cannot be grown at Wakehurst. They can, however, be seen in our conservatories at Kew.

ROCKY MOUNTAINS

Dominated by coniferous forest in which the mixture of species changes with increasing altitude. Ponderosa pine and scrub oak in the foothills give way to forests of mountain and sub-alpine species.

Engelmann spruce (*Picea engelmannii*) thrives in cold humid conditions and grows in the Rockies up to the tree line. The wood is used for sounding boards in pianos and violins.

CANADIAN

Sweeps across the north of the continent just south of the vast, cold, tundra plain. It has a harsh climate, locked in snow and ice for eight months every year. These forests are dominated by conifers with paper birch, quaking aspen and balsam poplar along the southern flanks of the province.

Tamarack (*Larix laricina*) is an extremely hardy tree found throughout the north-western forest. It is an important tree for wildlife and has very durable timber.

onifer woodland is the most extensive forest in the world, covering vast areas of North America, northern Europe and Asia – even larger than the area covered by tropical rainforest. Conifers, with their short branches and waxy leaves, are well able to withstand the long winters of heavy snow and drying winds found here and on mountain slopes where bands of conifers are an important winter refuge for animals.

In North America the northern conifer forest is dominated by spruces with pines, fir and patches of tamarack. Further south, the Pacific coast is drenched in rain and mist, supporting a belt of temperate rainforest of huge ancient evergreens. In the deep southern USA swamplands, such as Okefenokee Swamp, swamp cypress dominates a rich habitat supporting dense growths of epiphytes. In Europe's northern forests, Scots pine and spruces are the most important trees.

Wakehurst's **PINETUM** shows the variation to be found in all the major groups of conifers, particularly firs and spruces. Conifers are also important elements of the geographic plant collections in the woodlands and as ornamental trees around the **MANSION**.

COLLECTING CONIFER DIVERSITY

A wide variety of conifers is found on high tropical mountains and on the islands of South-East Asia. A recent expedition to Taiwan, for example (right), returned with an amazing diversity of conifer species which are being added to our collections at Kew and Wakehurst Place.

An ancient group of trees thrives in the Pinetum

CONIFERS

ANCIENT AND RELICT CONIFERS

The first time anyone saw a dawn redwood (*Metasequoia glyptostroboides*) it was as a fossil, found in 1941. But only a few years later it was found growing in the wild in western China. And in 1995 an Australian botanist discovered a new species of conifer, the Wollemi pine, growing in a deep gorge near Sydney, which looks almost identical to fossils from Jurassic times, when dinosaurs roamed the Earth.

Conifers are an ancient group which appeared before the flowering plants. There are fewer species of conifer alive today than in the geological past and many of these are close to extinction. Some survive in a very limited number of locations, perhaps places where there has been little geological upheaval or climatic change; or where there is little human interference. *Abies beshanzuensis*, a silver fir, is found on a single mountain top in China and only five trees remain.

IMPROVING THE CHRISTMAS TREE

Probably the most familiar conifer is the traditional Christmas tree, the Norway spruce. We are working with local foresters to broaden the range of conifers used as Christmas trees. Many not currently used may be more suitable than Norway spruce, for example by retaining their needles for longer. We are identifying these species and investigating growing methods. Trees are usually available from the Kew and Wakehurst Shops at Christmas time.

Cones from Pinus coulterii

RECORD BREAKING CONIFERS

Among conifers are the world's oldest and largest living things. The bristle-cone pines (*Pinus longaeva*, left) of Nevada, Utah and eastern California are believed to live more than 4,700 years. But they are youngsters compared with a huon pine (*Lagarostrobus franklinii*) in Tasmania, which is believed to be at least 10 times this age.

The most massive living things are the wellingtonias (*Sequoiadendron giganteum*) of North America's Pacific coast. The largest have been given names such as 'General Sherman' (83 metres tall, 24 metres across at head-height). Their thick fibrous bark (above) shields them against forest fires. Coast redwoods (*Sequoia sempervirens*) are even taller, but with less massive trunks.

WOODLAND LAYERS

In summer, the leafy branches of mature oaks and other large trees form an unbroken layer across the top of the wood. Where this canopy thins there is enough light for the understorey of smaller woodland trees – hazel, birch, holly and yew; and shrubs – hawthorn, bramble and dog rose, interwoven with climbers such as clematis and honeysuckle. In deciduous woods a tremendous diversity of wild flowers flourishes in early spring, before the trees have re-grown all their leaves. Wood anemones, primroses, bluebells, wood sorrel and dogs mercury thrive. The ancient wildwood was dense and shady. But humans learned that wood could be harvested by cutting the main shoots of the trees and allowing more to grow up from the stumps. This kept woodland open, allowing understorey plants and wildflowers a roothold.

FALLING FOR AUTUMN

In regions such as southern Europe, with mild frost-free winters, woodland is dominated by a profusion of conifers and evergreen broadleaf species, such as evergreen oaks. Deciduous trees lose their leaves in winter to avoid damage by cold and frost; in warmer areas species that retain their leaves have the advantage as they can grow throughout the year. Botanists believe the earliest broadleaved trees were evergreen. The evolution of deciduous species was a later adaptation involved with the colonisation of colder climates.

WEALDEN WOODS ◆

The plant collections at Wakehurst are set amongst one of the finest woodlands of southern England. As well as being beautiful, these woods have great scientific importance. Their long and unspoilt history means they offer a diversity of habitats for native plants and animals that have disappeared from other parts of South-East England. They also provide ideal conditions for growing some of Kew's scientific collections of temperate trees and shrubs from around the world.

REPLANTING WAKEHURST

Astonishingly, visitors will find it hard to see any traces of the two fierce storms that hit southern England in 1987 and 1990, even though we lost more than 15,000 trees.

Once we had recovered from the shock and the sadness of losing so many old favourites, we realised that every cloud has a silver lining. Satisfyingly there is now little evidence of the storms and replanting is giving us the opportunity to refresh the collections. We are planting new trees grown from seed collected from known sources on Kew expeditions, in arrangements that reflect the natural distributions of the species.

Replanting will continue for some time and we hope you will want to return to Wakehurst regularly to see the new species we are adding and to watch the collections take shape. Eventually you will be able to walk through the temperate woodlands of the world, starting with the Asian collections in WESTWOOD VALLEY, the Americas in HORSEBRIDGE WOOD, Southern Hemisphere trees in COATES' WOOD and European and Near-Eastern collections in BLOOMER'S VALLEY.

THE WEALD AND THE WORLD

The High Weald stretches from Kent to Hampshire. In many places the soils are too poor for intensive farming and the landscape too hilly and inaccessible for development – this was one of the last areas of England to be permanently settled by humans. So the Weald has been left with more woodland than many other areas – it has 20 per cent woodland cover, a little more than double the national average.

These woods were once part of a great forest which, in Roman times, would have extended from Kent to Hampshire and which probably originated from the ancient wildwood that covered Britain after the last ice age, ten thousand years ago. Before humans, such woodlands would have extended in a broad belt right across Europe and Asia in one direction and North America in the other. Further north, where the climate is harsher and the growing season shorter, oak, ash, beech and lime give way to birch, willow and poplar, followed by the vast dark forests of evergreen conifers.

Kew

THE WEALD

Wakehurst

*T*he combination of woodland, wetlands and meadows makes the Wakehurst Place estate one of the most important conservation sites in South-East England. This kind of landscape, offering a huge variety of habitats for wildlife, was once common. Now much has vanished under pressure from more intensive agriculture and urban development. **THE LODER VALLEY NATURE RESERVE**, *part of the Wakehurst Place estate and managed by us, preserves these important habitats and offers a home for a rich diversity of native plants and animals.*

THE LODER VALLEY NATURE RESERVE

The LODER VALLEY NATURE RESERVE *is on the south-western edge of the Wakehurst estate and is an area of 48 hectares dedicated to the conservation of the plants and animals of the Weald. Fine views across the Reserve can be seen from the Wakehurst Place boundary above the* WESTWOOD VALLEY *and* WETLAND CONSERVATION AREA*. The Reserve includes a 16 hectare branch of the Ardingly Reservoir and contains a rich variety of woodland, wetland and meadow habitats. The* WETLAND CONSERVATION AREA *at the bottom of* WESTWOOD VALLEY *gives a good flavour of the variety of habitats in the Reserve itself and the nearby classroom allows school groups and students get the best from educational visits.*

Entry to the Reserve is restricted to reduce excessive disturbance to the plants and animals there. Permits can be obtained by applying to the Administrator at Wakehurst Place or to the WAKEHURST SHOP*.*

MEADOWLAND

Fragrant, herb-filled summer meadows were once widespread in South-East England but farming changed making meadows, and the plants that once grew in them, scarce. So the meadows in the **LODER VALLEY RESERVE** are an important refuge, in places unchanged for over 30 years. Meadows are not natural.

The richness of their wild flowers depends on grazing, or mowing at certain times of year for haymaking. This keeps the grass short, allowing wildflowers to take hold. The mixture of species in an old meadow will depend partly on the nature of the soil and partly on what time of year the meadow is grazed or cut as different species of plants flower and set seed at different times of the year.

The beautiful Hanging Meadow in the Reserve is managed to increase the diversity of plant species.

It now supports well over 100 species, including old favourites such as oxeye daisy, lady's smock, bird's-foot trefoil, ragged robin and two species of orchid. Old meadows such as this deserve protection for the huge diversity of plants, insects and bird life they support.

WETLANDS &
MEADOWS

WETLAND

Rivers, streams, ponds, lakes, marshes and ditches were once common in Sussex. Flood control schemes and drainage for agriculture mean such habitats are now rare but Wakehurst Place and the Loder Valley Reserve retain a variety of wetland habitats from marshland to open water – each with characteristic plant and animal life.

Ghylls – deep, steep-sided valleys with wet, clayey soil – are particularly characteristic of the Weald. Wakehurst Place has many examples of ghyll woodland, in which many rare species of non-flowering plants – mosses, liverworts and lichens – find ideal growing conditions.

Almost half of all the plant species known to be endangered in Britain are wetland species and, in all, more than 500 species of plant and animal depend on freshwater habitats.

WOODLAND PRODUCTS

The traditional trug (top left) is made with a steamed ash or chestnut frame and cleft willow for strength and lightness. There has been a strong revival of interest in wood carving and turning (top right), which often makes use of waste wood. Hurdles (lower left) were a common form of portable fencing made of poles of oak, ash, willow or chestnut. Hazel hurdles are particularly strong, durable, light and portable, traditionally used for sheep-folding and now fashionable as garden screens. Bodgers (lower right) are skilled wood turners who produce chair legs and spindles on a simple pole-lathe. A new generation has revived the skill, using a range of woods.

*U*ntil early this century people relied on woodlands to provide the materials to make many every-day items: baskets, furniture, fencing, tools and fuel. Managing the woodlands to provide the materials, and the skills involved in producing the items, were important elements of the economy in areas such as the Weald.

The regular cutting of coppice woodland and clearing of under-growth let in the light and allowed wild flowers such as bluebells to establish on the woodland floor. But in modern times demand for woodland products has fallen. Traditional skills have been lost and woodlands neglected. Tree cover thickens, brambles and other scrubby shrubs invade, creating dense shade and causing a decline in many species of plants and animals.

At Wakehurst, we manage much of our woodland in the tradi-tional way to maximise its economic value while conserving its rich biological heritage. We also work to help keep traditional woodland management and craft skills alive, helping to promote demand for traditional woodland products – creating an econ-omic climate which encourages other woodland owners to manage their woodlands to help rural economies and conservation.

Harvesting can preserve the diversity of trees, shrubs and wild flowers in woods

LIVING RESOURCE

COPPICING & CHARCOAL PRODUCTION

Next time you are enjoying a summer barbecue, stop and think where the charcoal you are burning comes from. Chances are it will be imported, and it is quite likely to have come from unsustainable harvesting from tropical forests or mangrove swamps.

At Wakehurst we produce Bar B Kew Charcoal from coppiced woodland. Hardwood charcoal such as this is particularly good for barbecues because of its high carbon content, which makes it easy to light and quick to reach cooking temperature.

Coppicing involves cutting trees and shrubs to the ground and regularly harvesting the shoots which regrow from the stumps and roots. Some trees are retained to supply larger timber. Many native British species can be harvested in this way, the time between cuts depending on the species and the product. Hazel is coppiced every 7 to 10 years for pea sticks, bean poles, thatching spars, hurdles and fuel; sweet chestnut every 15 years for fencing; oak every 25 to 35 years for firewood and charcoal. Alder, beech, birch, field maple, small-leaved lime, sycamore, willow and wych elm are also important coppice trees in Britain. Coppicing benefits wild flowers such as bluebells, wood anemones, primroses and violets. But some birds, and insects such as white admiral butterflies, need the deep shade and cover of neglected woodland so we take care to retain a good balance of habitats.

CONSERVE WHEN YOU BUY

By purchasing products made from sustainably managed English woodlands you can help increase the economic viability of traditional skills, revive local rural economies and contribute to the conservation of wildlife.

BAR-B KEW charcoal

ROYAL BOTANIC GARDENS KEW

English Hardwood Charcoal produced by traditional skills from sustainably managed coppiced woodlands at Wakehurst Place

The Wakehurst estate contains a unique combination of woodland, meadow and wetland, which we can manage to provide ideal conditions for some of Britain's rarest plant species. Some of these are plants which were once more widespread but whose habitats have disappeared because of agricultural or building development. Others are rare because they are adapted to highly specialised conditions. Part of Wakehurst has been declared a Site of Special Scientific Interest because of its unique communities of mosses, liverworts and ferns, found in few other places in Britain.

TREES

We are also involved with English Nature's Species Recovery Programmes for some of Britain's rarest tree species, including Plymouth pear (Pyrus cordata), found at only two locations in Devon and Cornwall; rare species of native whitebeams, including Sorbus leyana and S. anglica; and black poplar (Populus nigra subsp. betulifolia), our rarest native timber tree. We are researching ways of propagating these plants, increasing their natural variability, and reintroducing them to suitable habitats.

ORCHID CONSERVATION

The woodlands and fields of Wakehurst Place are home to at least six different species of native orchids. The grassy banks in the area known as the SLIPS, and the woodlands of the WESTWOOD VALLEY are the best places to look. In April a number of wild flowers appear in the grass between the magnolia trees at the top of the SLIPS, including the green winged orchid (*Orchis morio*), one of the earliest native orchids into flower. It is followed in early May by the taller Jersey orchid (*O. laxiflora,* below left). These plants were raised from seeds in the laboratories at Kew as part of the Sainsbury Orchid Conservation Project and this species was one of the first to be successfully transferred from the greenhouses to the open gardens. This has helped us understand more about how to introduce rare orchids back into suitable natural habitats. Spotted orchids (*Dactylorhiza fuchsii*) also grow here but they tend to flower later when the grass is longer, so they are less easily seen.

In the woodlands of WESTWOOD VALLEY grow two species of native helleborine: broad leaved or common helleborine (*Epipactis helleborine*) with greenish purple flowers, which grows best in dark dingy corners and flowers well into September; and the violet helleborine (*E. purpurata,* below). However you are more likely to see the yellowish green flowers of common twayblade (*Listera ovata*) in dappled shade near the paths; or more of the spotted orchids, which flourish in many habitats including woodland, downland and marshy areas.

MOSSES, FERNS AND LIVERWORTS

They may not bear striking flowers but mosses, liverworts and ferns have a beauty all their own. And among them are some of Britain's rarest plant species. Mosses do not have true roots and have to absorb moisture over their entire surface, so they can only grow in moist habitats. Wakehurst's woods have many damp places which are ideal. Unlike most other plants, mosses grow more quickly in winter because that is when there is most moisture. Mosses are often the first plants to colonise bare ground on poor soil, stabilising it and trapping moisture which allows other plants to gain a root-hold. They can also grow over rocks and tree roots. At Wakehurst a number of species grow on the rocks along the ROCK WALK.

The sandstone outcrops in Wakehurst's damp, shady woodlands are among the top ten sites for conservation of mosses, liverworts and ferns, which all need constant moisture to survive. Wakehurst is one of the key sites in English Nature's Species Recovery Programmes for some of them. At Wakehurst we are working with English Nature to support four key species: *Fissidens exiguus* and *Orthodontum gracile* (mosses), *Pallavicinia lyellii* (a liverwort) and *Trichomanes speciosum* (Killarney fern).

NATIVE PLANTS

Conservation of native plants at Wakehurst Place

NATIVE ANIMALS

BADGERS

Badgers are shy and are only active from twilight and through the night. But they are social animals, living in groups which vary in size according to the amount of food available and suitable terrain for digging setts. These underground labyrinths can be used over hundreds of years by many generations and are always spotlessly clean. In late autumn the badgers line their deep winter quarters with leaves which generate warmth as they decay. The main sett is used for breeding, annexes provide refuges while out on forays. Badgers can mate at any time of year but the embryos remain in 'suspended animation' until early December when they start to grow rapidly. Baby badgers are born in February and make their way above ground for their first adventures in April or early May.

Wakehurst's woodlands are ideal for badgers and setts on the estate are regularly watched and monitored by members of local wildlife and badger protection groups and by local members of the Friends of the Royal Botanic Gardens, Kew.

DORMOUSE

At Wakehurst we are helping English Nature's Species Recovery Programme for the dormouse. In parts of the woodland we ensure the coppice cycle is long enough (10 to 15 years) to allow food plants such as hazel to flower and fruit and bramble to invade to provide the dense cover it needs. Dormouse nest boxes have also been placed and these are monitored to help build up a picture of the national population.

The dormouse is named for its long winter hibernation. It stays alive by very slowly digesting fat stored up during the autumn. Woodland with a good supply of seeds, berries, nuts and insects is essential for its survival.

BIRDS

Wakehurst is a stopping off point for migrating birds and an important breeding site for visiting species. Restoring the woodland areas and reintroducing traditional management techniques have seen the return of nightingales after an absence of more than 25 years. A feature of birds in the Gardens is their tameness. Pheasants, and even chaffinches and robins have been known to feed out of visitors hands.

Our wetland areas are particularly important for birds. Look out for kingfishers and herons around WESTWOOD LAKE and the WETLAND CONSERVATION AREA. Great crested grebes breed in the LODER VALLEY RESERVE while sandpipers and Canada geese are regular visitors. Cormorants come to the reservoir to feed while ospreys and hobbies have been seen during summer. Kestrels regularly patrol the meadows and warblers frequent the mature woodlands.

f you want to conserve animals, you must conserve the habitats in which they live and the plants on which, ultimately, all animals depend. The gardens, woodlands, meadows and wetlands of the Wakehurst estate provide a good diversity of habitats for a wide variety of Britain's native wild animals – from much-loved mammals such as badgers to insects such as dragonflies and butterflies which play vital roles in the ecosystem. At Wakehurst we are working closely with local and national conservation groups to develop ways of managing the estate that also benefit our wildlife.

BATS

Dead and hollow trees were one of the most important roosting places for bats but in many commercial woodlands these are removed. Some species of bat have halved in numbers this century. In some of the woodlands at Wakehurst we leave dead trees to decay naturally to provide a habitat for bats and other woodland wildlife. Bat boxes have also been installed. Wakehurst's bats include the long eared bat, pipistrelle, serontine and noctule. Bats can live up to 25 years in the wild.

DRAGONFLIES

Twenty different species of dragon fly have been seen at Wakehurst, four of which are among the rarest in the country because their habitats are disappearing. They need vegetation close to the water's edge to provide cover while preying on other insects during the day, together with woodland further away where they feed in the evenings. Stretches of water are vital for breeding. Wakehurst, particularly the WETLAND CONSERVATION AREA in the WESTWOOD VALLEY, is therefore an ideal habitat.

Some grass areas close to the ponds in the formal areas of the gardens are left uncut to provide feeding sites for dragonflies. In some areas, trees are pruned to increase the amount of sun falling on the water plants.

Different species of fungi live on different materials. Some are able to overcome the natural defences of living plants and so cause diseases and a few are even able to decay living timber although in most cases woodland trees have to be suffering from some form of stress – perhaps drought or shade from a taller tree – before such fungi can do serious damage.

Kew's mycologists – scientists who specialise in fungi – are investigating the role of fungi in recycling nutrients in woodlands and other natural systems. But they are discovering that, just like plants, some species of fungi can become endangered when their habitats disappear. At Wakehurst we try to help fungi, for example by leaving fallen trees untouched in some parts of the woodlands so that the nutrients in the timber can be returned to the soil for future

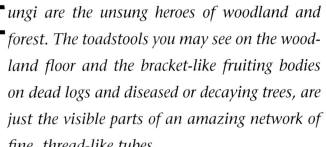

FUNGI

The lichens you see encrusting the bark of some trees are also fungi but with an algal partner. The fungus absorbs minerals and holds fast to hard surfaces, the alga converts solar energy into food for the fungus.

ungi are the unsung heroes of woodland and forest. The toadstools you may see on the woodland floor and the bracket-like fruiting bodies on dead logs and diseased or decaying trees, are just the visible parts of an amazing network of fine, thread-like tubes.

Toadstools and other fruiting bodies are the reproductive organs – like the flowers of a green plant. But unlike plants, fungi cannot make their own food from sunlight. Instead their vast network of microscopic threads – hyphae – produce digestive enzymes which break down organic material such as leaves or wood. If it were not for them, and countless microbes, Wakehurst would be buried under a mountain of plant debris.

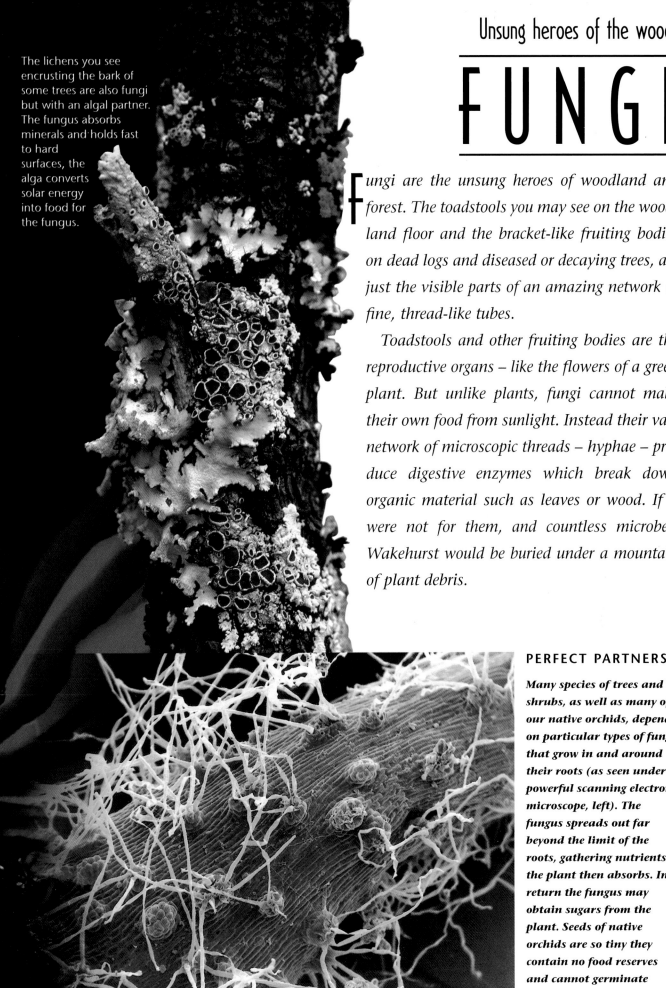

PERFECT PARTNERS

Many species of trees and shrubs, as well as many of our native orchids, depend on particular types of fungi that grow in and around their roots (as seen under a powerful scanning electron microscope, left). The fungus spreads out far beyond the limit of the roots, gathering nutrients the plant then absorbs. In return the fungus may obtain sugars from the plant. Seeds of native orchids are so tiny they contain no food reserves and cannot germinate unless the right kind of fungus is present.

*K*nowing more about where plants come from and the kinds of habitats they enjoy in the wild, can help you to choose the most suitable plants for your own garden. Many of the ornamental plantings have been designed to give you ideas to try out. We have given particular thought to providing winter colour, growing plants on exposed sites, using texture and colour to create effect and planting around water or in waterlogged places. Throughout the gardens we have used some particularly fine plants from around the world, which deserve to be more widely grown.

NATIONAL COLLECTIONS

Wakehurst Place is home to four National Plant Collections. These are recognised by the National Council for the Conservation of Plants and Gardens which means they are as comprehensive a collection of the species and cultivars of that particular group of plants as possible. The collections are available to botanists and horticulturists for research and are a valuable resource for gardeners because the full range of characteristics of the group of plants can be compared. The four collections are: birch (**BETHLEHEM WOOD**), southern beech (**COATES' WOOD**), hypericum and skimmia (**SPECIMEN BEDS** near the Mansion).

PLANTS FOR EXPOSED PLACES

The TONY SCHILLING ASIAN HEATH GARDEN *shows many kinds of plants that can be used on exposed sites. All these plants live high up in the mountains of Asia. Their dwarf, rounded forms of growth are an adaptation to almost constant wind but this shape also makes them ideal for smaller gardens. One bed shows cultivated varieties of dwarf rhododendrons bred from Asian heathland species. You can also see the kinds of natural plant association formed, with shrubs and small trees such as juniper, cotoneaster, potentilla, birch, rowan and berberis. The garden is named after the Deputy Curator of Wakehurst from 1967 to 1991.*

WALLED GARDEN STYLE

There are two distinctive **WALLED GARDENS**. The Sir Henry Price Garden commemorates a former owner of Wakehurst, who did much to build up the collections of rare and unusual plants. Informal groups of plants are arranged within a formal setting. It has a very restful atmosphere created by limiting the plants to those with foliage and flowers in pastel shades – grey and silver-leaved artemisias and lavenders create a foil for blue, lilac and pink flowered species.

The adjacent Pleasaunce is a formal area with a pool and fountain where we create spring and summer displays using unusual combinations of plants.

AUTUMN AND WINTER FORM AND COLOUR

The **WINTER GARDEN**, on the western side of the Mansion, shows how plants can provide interest through the normally drab months in your garden. Plants commonly grown for their winter colour are combined with less well-known species. The brightly coloured stems of the dogwoods (*Cornus* species) and willows (*Salix*) for example, contrast with the dried leaves of ornamental grasses such as *Molinia caerulea* 'Variegata'. Unusual species of viburnums and witch hazels come into flower from January. In the **SLIPS** masses of Himalayan bistort (*Persicaria affine*) show off their superb russet tints in autumn.

Wakehurst's autumn colour is often spectacular. Colours range from apricot *Sorbus* 'Embley' through scarlet and orange *Enkianthus perrulatus* and *Acer palmatum* cultivars to the crimson *Acer* 'October Glory', all in the area close to the **GARDEN ENTRANCE**. By the south-west corner of the **MANSION POND** you can see *Betula nigra* 'Wakehurst', a recently named and outstanding variety of river birch with exceptional bark and wonderful golden-yellow autumn colour.

Our plantings can help you identify ideas to try in your own garden

ORNAMENTALS

THE MILLENNIUM

WHAT IS A SEED BANK?

Seed banks are the most effective and economical means of conserving plants when their natural habitats are likely to be lost and they allow a large amount of genetic diversity to be stored in a relatively small space. Seed is collected from the wild, cleaned, dried carefully and then stored in the Bank at sub-zero temperatures. In these conditions seed can retain its ability to germinate for decades, perhaps centuries. Seed samples can be distributed to scientists and conservationists around the world to be used for reintroduction to the wild or for research to find new ways for plants to benefit society. Seed banks are, ultimately, the last line of defence against extinction.

WHAT KINDS OF SEED ARE STORED?

The dry tropics and sub-tropics are among the most threatened environments on Earth. They are home to an immense variety of plant life, including many species used by the people who live in these regions. With our overseas partners, we target such species for collection, alongside others identified as being particularly rare or under threat.

Plants from the wetter regions of the tropics often have seeds which are killed by drying or cooling. We are developing alternative methods of conserving these species, for example by pre-serving embryos removed from the seed.

In the Seed Bank, our collections are stored at a freezing cold -20 degrees Celsius.

Storing seeds to save species from extinction

SEED BANK

THE MILLENNIUM SEED BANK

The Millennium Seed Bank project will aim to collect and conserve seed from all the UK's native flowering plant species by the year 2000 and from 10 per cent of the world's species, concentrating on the dry tropical regions, by 2010. The project will be a partnership between Kew and similar organisations in other countries and much of the collecting overseas will be done in collaboration with local botanists, who would be able to receive training at the Millennium Seed Bank. Seeds will be held in trust for the countries in which they were collected and advice and training will be given to help these countries develop their own seed storage facilities and conserve their own plants.

Collection of seeds from the UK flora will be aided by volunteers from local wildlife organisations.

THE BUILDING

The Millennium Seed Bank, which is due to open by the year 2000 and which is designed to last at least 500 years, will provide space to house thousands of seed samples in a large underground vault as well as including advanced seed processing and research facilities. There will also be public walkways so that you will be able to see the scientists at work and interactive exhibits demonstrating the importance of our seed conservation programme.

*S*eeds are miracles of packaging. They contain all the genetic information needed to create the next generation of plants. Seed of many species in temperate parts of the world, such as the British Isles, are shed in autumn, lie dormant over winter and germinate when they sense the longer days and warmer weather of spring. But seeds can lie dormant for much longer. Seeds of some desert species can lie in the soil for many years until the rains come, then burst into spectacular, colourful, life.

For the last 20 years, we have been using this natural ability of seeds to survive for long periods by storing seed in our Seed Bank at Wakehurst, thus helping to conserve some of the world's rich and varied plant life. The Millennium Seed Bank project marks a dramatic expansion in the scale of this work, and is the most exciting and ambitious conservation project we have ever undertaken. The Millennium Seed Bank will safeguard species against extinction for many generations and will provide a unique resource for the world.

FUNDING THE MILLENNIUM SEED BANK

In December 1995 the Millennium Seed Bank project received a grant of £21 million from the Millennium Commission, which distributes money raised from the National Lottery. The Millennium Seed Bank is one of the few to be designated as a Landmark Project,

recognised as having particular significance for the next thousand years. In total the project will cost around £76 million. We anticipate that much of the cost of collecting and researching seeds from overseas will be met through international donor agencies.

You can help us complete this globally significant project. £7·3 million is being raised in partnerships with corporate sponsors and from public appeals. Current details of how to contribute are available on separate leaflets, or you can make a credit card donation on 0973 10 2000.

PHOTOGRAPHIC CREDITS

All images © Trustees, Royal Botanic Gardens Kew except:

COVER: butterfly (P Gasson/RBG Kew)

PLANTS AND PLACES: world map (based on © Mountain High Maps).

AMERICAN DREAM: birch (H McAllister); tamarack (John Shaw/NHPA); redwood (Heather Angel); map of North America (based on © Mountain High Maps).

ASIA: Nepal (Bob Gibbons/Ardea).

SOUTHERN HEMISPHERE: New Zealand forest (Jean-Paul Ferrero/Ardea); hebe (Heather Angel); southern beech (D Parer & E Parer-Cook/Ardea).

CONIFERS: Canada treescape (Francisco Futil/Bruce Coleman); bristlecone pine (Wardene Weisse/ Ardea); living fossil (based on © John Mason/Ardea).

WEALDEN WOODS: map (based on © Mountain High Maps); oakwood (Stephen Dalton/NHPA); Autumn leaves (David Crawford).

WETLANDS AND MEADOWS: all photographs © Stephen Dalton/NHPA.

LIVING RESOURCE: trug maker, wood-carver (Collections/Ben Boswell); hurdle maker (Jacqui Hurst); coppicing (John Mason/Ardea); charcoal making (Stephen Dalton/NHPA).

NATIVE PLANTS: mossy pool (Stephen Dalton/NHPA); Jersey orchid, violet helleborine (P Gasson/RBG Kew).

NATIVE ANIMALS: dormouse, spotted flycatcher, kingfisher, bat, dragonfly (Stephen Dalton/NHPA).

FUNGI: lichen (Heather Angel); yellow toadstool (David Crawford)

PICTURE RESEARCH: Anne-Marie Ehrlich

OTHER CREDITS

Text by Spence Gunn, editor, 'Kew' magazine
Design concept by John Willis Fleming
Design by John Willis Fleming, John Stone and members of the Media Resources team, RBG Kew
All images scanned using Kodak PhotoCD Technology; Scanning by B&S Visual Technologies, Glasgow
Repro of films for press by Magnet Harlequin, Uxbridge
Printed by HMSO Norwich Print Services

Set in Stone Sans and Stone Serif

ISBN 1 900347 03 2

GENERAL INFORMATION – WAKEHURST PLACE

Photography, Painting etc

Any commercial work needs prior agreement. Contact 0181 332 5607 for more information.

Wheelchairs

Please telephone 0181 332 5121 for details. Please note that while much of the upper Garden is accessible there are steep paths unsuitable for wheelchairs beyond the upper part of Westwood Valley through to Bethlehem Wood. These are indicated on the map inside the front cover and on the map boards throughout the Gardens.

Food and Drink

The Stable Restaurant is open throughout the year selling tea, coffee, cold drinks and a selection of snacks, salads and hot meals (tel 01444 894040). Group catering should be booked in advance.

Wakehurst Shop

Open daily from 10am selling a variety of books, cards, stationery, souvenirs, film and stamps. BAR-B-Kew charcoal, made from sustainable resources on the Wakehurst estate is available in spring and summer, Christmas trees from the first weekend in December, tel 01444 894073.

Guided tours and trails

Guided Tours leave the Mansion at 11.30am and 2.30pm in the summer (winter 2pm only) and may be booked in advance from the Rangers Office (01444 894070), maximum 25 per group. Leaflets showing the Dinosaur and Birch Trails are available from the Giftshop for a small charge. There are also various information sheets.

Groups

Groups of ten or more paying visitors may obtain a discount on receipt of advance payment. For details and an application form, please contact the Enquiry Unit, Tel 01444 894067. Group catering, if needed, should be booked in advance.

School Parties

Schools and colleges may make arrangements to use our Field Studies Centre, tel 01444 894094. A teacher training programme is also available.

Getting to Wakehurst

Wakehurst Place is 15 minutes from Junction 10 on the M23, just north of Ardingly on the B2028. The nearest station is Haywards Heath, 6 miles by taxi or by 472 bus (not Sundays) which runs from Crawley to Haywards Heath and return. Bus 772 runs from Crawley via Wakehurst and Haywards Heath to Brighton and return on Sundays and Bank Holidays. Call 01273 886200 for information about the 772 and 01293 414081 for the 472.

Opening Times and admission prices

The gardens are open from 10 am every day except Christmas Day and New Year's Day. Closing time varies according to time of year. For current times and prices please telephone 01444 894066

Please Care For The Gardens

To protect both the enjoyment of visitors and the plant collections, please observe the folowing: visitors are asked not to handle the plants or climb trees; bicycles, trikes, ball games, sports, musical instruments and radios are not permitted; no dogs are allowed, except Guide Dogs.

£2 off Entry Fee

Please hand the completed form to the Ticket Office to obtain £2 off the normal entry fee on your next visit.

To the Ticket Officer: When completed and signed this voucher entitles the bearer to obtain entry to Kew Gardens or Wakehurst Place at £2 off the normal entry fee during normal opening hours. It may not be exchanged for cash and cannot be used with any other offer.

Name

Address

Postcode

Date Guidebook purchased

Date of this visit

signed

Data Protection: We may from time to time send you information about RBG Kew and its activities. If you would prefer not to receive such information, please tick

---

GENERAL INFORMATION – WAKEHURST PLACE continued

ENTRY TO LODER VALLEY RESERVE

At least 24 hrs notice is needed. Permits obtainable from the Shop or Administration Office (01444 894067). (Loder Valley Information Pack available from the shop).

FOR MORE INFORMATION

Wakehurst Place, Ardingly, West Sussex RH17 6TN Telephone 01444 894066 (recorded information given when office staff unavailable).
If you have access to the Internet, visit our Web Site on http://www.rbgkew.org.uk

---

JOIN THE FRIENDS OF THE ROYAL BOTANIC GARDENS, KEW

If you are interested in learning more about the Royal Botanic Gardens at Kew and Wakehurst Place, why not join the Friends of Kew? You will be helping to support our vital botanical research and conservation work and in return we give you unlimited free entry to the Gardens, free guest passes for your friends, a superb colour magazine and the chance to join in a wide range of interesting Friends events at both Kew and Wakehurst Place.

YOUR PASSPORT TO MAGNIFICENT GARDENS

Your Friends Membership Pass entitles you to free entry, throughout the year, to both Kew Gardens and Wakehurst Place – two of the world's greatest botanical garden where there is plenty to see throughout the year. Our Friends enjoy the opportunity to return regularly to watch how the Gardens change with the seasons, and to follow the development of the plant collections as new species and interpretive features are continually added. There is always something new to discover.
We have also negotiated free entry for our Friends to a number of other famous gardens throughout the country.

FREE PASSES FOR YOUR GUESTS

Kew and Wakehurst are wonderful places for a day out with friends and relations. Eace adult receives six free guest passes a year for use at Kew or Wakehurst Place. Even when you have used these up, each adult Friend can bring a guest at any time and the guest pays only the concessionary admission price to the Gardens.

FREE MAGAZINE

Kew, the Friends' high quality colour magazine, is published three times a year and mailed free to you when you become a Friend. It deals with the important environmental issues of the day in a lively, colourful and informative way, with articles from the world's leading botanists, horticulturists and conservationists. We cover the plants of the world, from tropical rainforest trees to the pot plants on your windowsill and each issue highlights a topical aspect of our work at Kew and Wakehurst. With the magazine you can also keep up to date with Friends fundraising programmes and get the first chance to book events at Kew and Wakehurst.

SPECIAL EVENTS

The Friends runs a full programme of events throughout the year including coffee mornings, lectures, guided garden tours, plant auctions and botanical and horticultural excursions, tours and holidays led by Kew experts.

SPECIAL SAVINGS

Friends can obtain discounts at the Kew and Wakehurst shops.

FUND-RAISING

Each Friends subscription helps to maintain the Gardens at Kew and Wakehurst and to fund our botanical research and conservation work. In addition Friends have raised funds for specific projects such as the conservation of endangered island plants and the construction of new features in the Gardens.

£5 off Friends Membership or £2 off Season Ticket

This coupon is worth £5 against your first years membership or renewal of membership of the Friends of the Royal Botanic Gardens, Kew, or £2 against payment for a season ticket. It is not exchang-able for cash and cannot be used in conjunction with any other offer.

NEW FRIENDS MEMBERSHIP OR SEASON TICKET

Enclose this coupon with your application and payment. Application forms are on your free Welcome to Kew leaflet or can be obtained from the ticket offices or from the Friends Help Desk in the Victoria Gate Visitor Centre at Kew or in the Mansion at Wakehurst Place, or by telephoning the Friends Office on 0181 332 5922.

GENERAL INFORMATION – KEW continued

KEW SHOPS

Kew has two shops, at Victoria Gate and near the Main Gate (currently in the Orangery but planned to move to the Nash Conservatory). A wide selection of books including those of horticultural and scientific interest is available, as well as Kew's range of china, stationery, toiletries and prints. In addition, the Victoria Gate Shop has a newly extended children's section including gifts and souvenirs.

Bar-B-Kew Charcoal, produced at Wakehurst Place is on sale in the spring and summer.

For further information on our shops and products and details of how to obtain these items by mail order, please telephone 0181 332 5653.

REFRESHMENTS (Summer)

There are three main restaurant facilities:

The Orangery, near the Main Gate, is open all year.

The Pavillion Restaurant, near the Pagoda and Temperate House, is our largest restaurant and is open from Spring to early Autumn.

The Bakery, between the Main Gate and Brentford Gate, pro-vides outdoor seating and a range of snacks and is also open seasonally.

Kiosks selling a range of ice-creams, drinks and snacks are located behind the Orangery (seasonal) and in the Victoria Gate Visitor Centre (year round).

For general enquiries or details of opening hours please con-tact the Catering Manager on 0181 332 5186.

For details of private catering within Kew Gardens, please phone 0181 332 5680.

EDUCATION

The Education Section provides a range of services and pro-grammes for both adults and schools. These include day-courses in aspects of gardening, INSET teacher training, outreach activities for schools, photography and painting courses and lecture programmes. For details of current and forthcoming activities, write for a brochure to either the Adult Education Section or the Schools Education Officer, Royal Botanic Gardens, Kew. Please enclose a large stamped addressed envelope.

VENUES FOR HIRE

Facilities at Kew are available for hire for private events includ-ing weddings. For details contact RBG Kew Enterprises on 0181 332 5617

SPECIAL EVENTS PROGRAMME

For details of Summer Jazz Concerts, Family Summer Picnic party, Spring Orchid Festival and special Christmas events, please contact 0181 332 5622

FURTHER SOURCES OF INFORMATION

A range of trails and information sheets, covering various aspects of the Gardens, is available from the Shop. If you have access to the Internet, visit our Web Site on http://www.rbgkew.org.uk

For further information about Kew please contact:

The Enquiry Unit, Royal Botanic Gardens, Kew Richmond Surrey TW9 3AB, Telephone: 0181 332 5622 (weekdays, 9am to 5pm). Because we receive so many calls on a wide variety of subjects we regret we cannot always provide an on the spot response. Admission times and prices are available quickly on 0181 940 1171 (24hr recorded information).

GENERAL INFORMATION - KEW

weekdays and from 4 pm to 7.30 pm on weekends and Public Holidays, dependent on the season, with last admissions half an hour earlier.

The Conservatories, Kew Gardens Gallery and Marianne North Gallery also open at 9.30 am. The closing time for Conservatories and Galleries is earlier than the Gardens. Galleries occasionally close at lunchtimes. In addition, Kew Gardens Gallery may be closed occasionally particularly on Saturday afternoons for private events.

For current opening times and admission prices telephone 0181 940 1171.

KEW PALACE AND QUEEN CHARLOTTE'S COTTAGE

These historic buildings lie within Kew Gardens but are administered separately by Historic Royal Palaces. For general enquiries and details of admission times and prices, please contact Historic Royal Palaces on 0181 781 9500.

PLEASE CARE FOR THE GARDENS

To protect both the enjoyment of visitors and the plant collections, please observe the following: visitors are asked not to handle the plants or climb trees; bicycles, trikes, ball games, sports, musical instruments and radios etc are not permitted; no dogs are allowed, except Guide Dogs.

PHOTOGRAPHY, PAINTING ETC

Permits are required for tripods or easels in the Conservatories (weekdays only to avoid congestion), contact 0181 332 5622. Any commercial work needs prior agreement – Contact 0181 332 5607.

WHEELCHAIRS

Wheelchairs can be borrowed; it is advisable to book them in advance. Please telephone 0181 332 5121 for details.

GROUP BOOKINGS

Contact the Enquiry Unit, Tel 0181 332 5622 for details.

GUIDED TOURS

One-hour introductory tours for individual visitors and small groups available from the Victoria Gate Visitor Centre for a small charge. Groups of 10 or more people should book a guide in advance. Early booking is advisable, especially during spring and summer. For details, contact the Guided Tours Co-ordinator, either by letter or by telephoning 0181 332 5633.

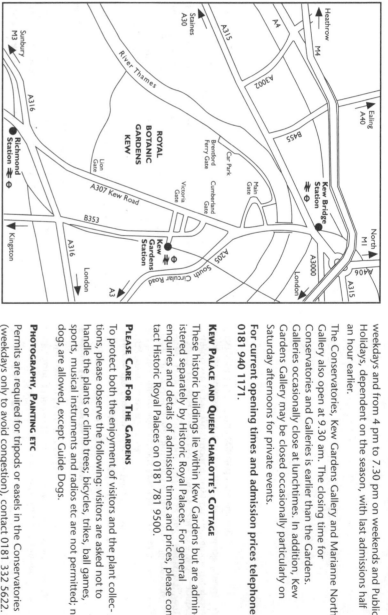

GETTING TO KEW

Bus: 65, 391, 267 and R68 (Sundays only).

Underground: Kew Gardens Station (District Line)

Rail: Kew Bridge Station (South West Trains, Waterloo line); Kew Gardens Station (North London Railways).

Passenger Boat Service: from Westminster, Putney or Hampton Court, Summer only. Tel: 0171 930 2062/4721.

Car: Parking around Kew Green (off South Circular Road, A205, just south of Kew Bridge), or in the Car Park, reached via Ferry Lane off Kew Green. Parking is also available on Kew Road, A307 (check restriction signs).

OPENING TIMES

Open daily except Christmas Day and New Year's Day, from 9.30 am. Closing times vary from about 4 pm to 6.30 pm on

OTHER CREDITS

Text by Spence Gunn, editor, 'Kew' magazine
Design concept by John Willis Fleming
Design by John Willis Fleming, John Stone and members of the Media Resources team, RBG Kew
All images scanned using Kodak PhotoCD Technology; Scanning by B&S Visual Technologies, Glasgow
Repro of films for press by Magnet Harlequin, Uxbridge
Printed by HMSO Norwich Print Services

Set in Stone Sans and Stone Serif

© Board of Trustees, Royal Botanic Gardens, Kew

ISBN 1 900347 03 2

TREES & WOODS

WOODLAND GARDEN IN SPRING

The WOODLAND GARDEN is planted to represent the change in vegetation between forests and mountain areas. Deciduous oaks and birches support climbers and provide shade for the lower layers of rhododendrons and maples, and for herbaceous plants such as hellebores, primulas and the North American trilliums.

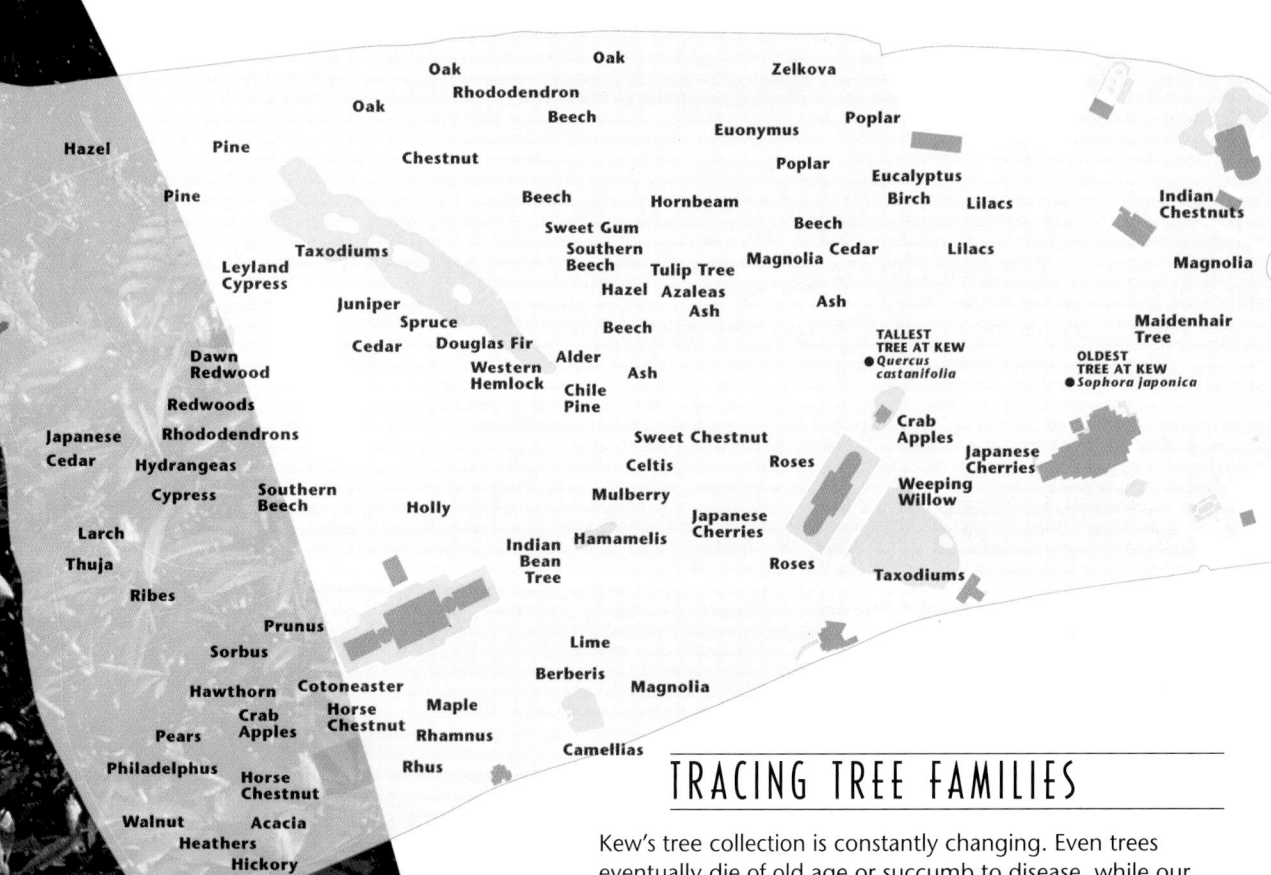

TRACING TREE FAMILIES

Kew's tree collection is constantly changing. Even trees eventually die of old age or succumb to disease, while our botanists and horticulturists are constantly bringing back interesting new or unusual species from overseas expeditions to add to the collections.

Closely related species of trees and shrubs tend to be planted close to each other at Kew, to reflect their relationships (map, above). Oaks, chestnuts and beeches are found along the northern flanks of the LAKE, for example; families of conifers north-east of QUEEN CHARLOTTE'S COTTAGE.

The aim of the collection is not only to represent as wide a range of species as possible but also to show the variation that can sometimes occur within individual species from different places. The result is a living library of the world's hardy trees and shrubs.

Most of the trees and shrubs are grown from seed collected in the wild, usually on joint expeditions with scientists in the country involved. Some seed is grown on the nurseries at Kew, some is stored for future use in Kew's Seed Bank and some is shared with other botanical organisations.

THE ORIGINS OF GARDEN VARIETIES

Some of the plantings within the Arboretum show the development of garden shrubs and their relationship to wild plants.

Azaleas, for example, were introduced as greenhouse plants from eastern North America in the 18th century but they became more popular as garden shrubs. Azaleas are all members of the genus *Rhododendron* and it is easy to see the similarity in their flowers. From the middle of the 1800s to the present, nurserymen and plant breeders have busily crossed many species and hybrids to produce the plants you can buy in a garden centre. In Kew's AZALEA GARDEN you can follow their development from the famous Ghent hybrids first grown in the 1820s to modern American hybrids.

In the nearby RHODODENDRON DELL you can see the natural diversity of wild rhododendron species from which such garden types have been raised. Kew's lilac, peony and philadelphus collections are also being developed to reflect the relationships between varieties bred by nurserymen and natural species.

Each species of tree, this is elm, has its own characteristic pattern of water conducting vessels in the woody tissues of the stems. The different arrangements of vessels and strengthening fibres determine the properties of the timber.

*Some areas of the
Arboretum are managed
to provide food and
shelter for butterflies,
such as this brimstone,
feeding on
a thistle*

*Kew's bluebell woods are among
the finest in the London area*

Kew's tranquil Arboretum contains Britain's most important collection of trees

TREES & WOODS

Trees capture our imagination in a way that no other organism can. The largest trees, the coast redwoods and wellingtonias (Sequoia sempervirens and Sequoiadendron giganteum) *are the largest living things on Earth. Sitting quietly in the middle of a wood or forest is perhaps when one feels closest to nature.*

Tree species have evolved many times in evolutionary history in a very large number of families of plants but they are all large perennial plants with woody stems. The difference between a tree and a shrub is simply a matter of scale.

Kew's tree collection has a long history. Great landscapers such as 'Capability' Brown and William Nesfield contributed to its underlying character but it does not take long to realise that the layout of trees and shrubs follows a pattern that reflects our interest in the family relationships between plants. The collection currently holds some 9,000 trees, representing more than 2,000 species and varieties, making it one of the world's most important fully documented living libraries of trees.

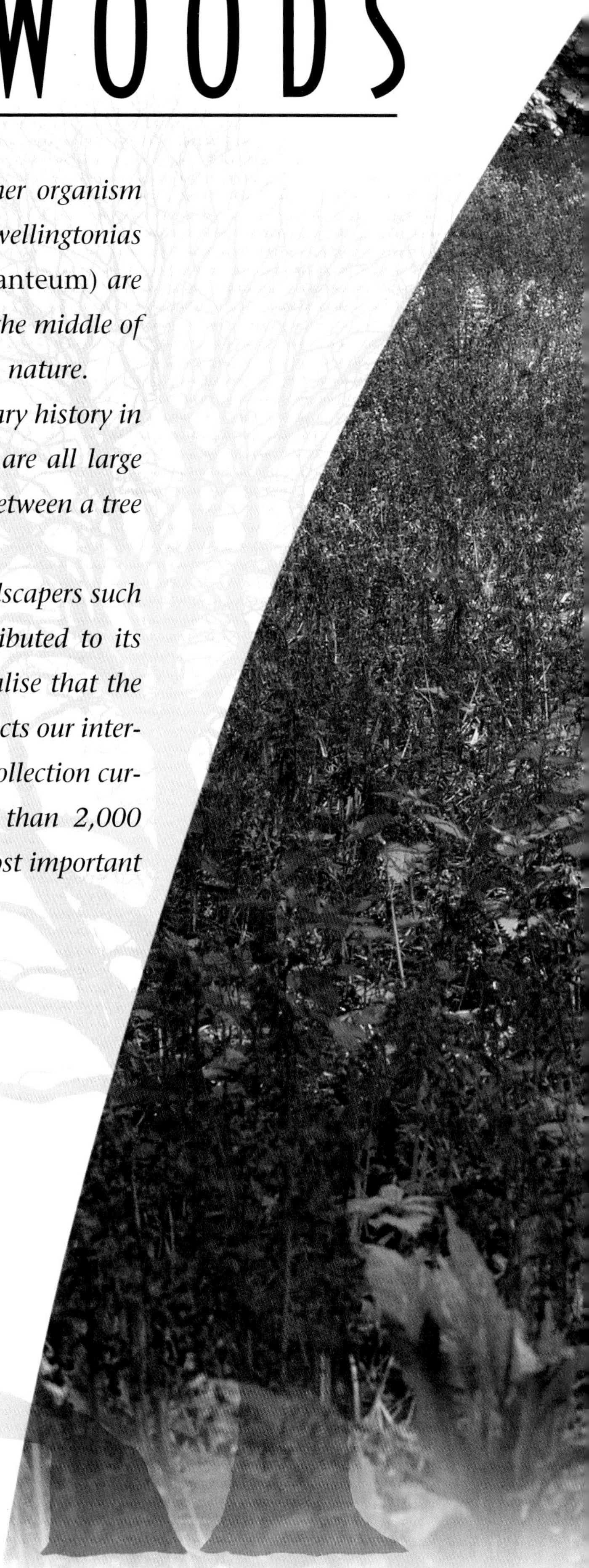

A magnificent chestnut-leaved oak (*Quercus castanifolia*, seen here in silhouette) behind the WATERLILY HOUSE is Kew's largest tree, 7.1 metres in girth and some 35 metres tall

The venerable *Sophora japonica* (seen here in silhouette) near the PRINCESS OF WALES CONSERVATORY, is one of the few trees to survive from the original plantings in 1759

ALTITUDE PLANTS

SURVIVING THE COLD

The **ALPINE HOUSE** (far left) is one of the treasures of the Gardens with a succession of beautiful, delicate alpine plants displaying their bright flowers throughout the year.

But these beauties have to be tough, too. In winter near the Poles the temperature can drop to -35 degrees Celsius and rarely rises above freezing. The short summer growing season may last only two months. On high mountains in the tropics plants must cope with temperatures that switch from below freezing at night to about 30 degrees Celsius during the day thanks to the thin, clear mountain air. You can see how some plants survive in Kew's **ALPINE HOUSE** and **ROCK GARDEN**.

Some are insulated with dense hairs, like the fur of an animal. The plant is warmed by the sun during the day and the hairs trap and retain the heat at night.

On tropical mountains, some species grow to gigantic proportions as a strategy to survive the night-time cold. Giant equatorial groundsels (*Senecio* species) and lobelias (such as *Lobelia keniensis,* left, from Mount Kenya) look quite unlike their tiny relatives familiar to gardeners. These giants are taller than a human and have thick layers of hairs and dead leaves around their stems as insulation – reducing heat loss at night and reflecting the intense sunlight at midday. Their size and layers of insulation mean they heat up slowly during the day and retain their heat right through the night – like botanical storage heaters. Some produce a special 'anti-freeze' liquid that surrounds the delicate growing bud. Others have hollow stems full of sugary liquid where ice can form, drawing water away from the plant tissues and so making them less likely to freeze.

HUGGING THE GROUND

The shape of low-growing alpine and tundra plants such as saxifrages (Saxifraga cochlearis, left) is an adaptation to avoid damage by strong winds. Dense rosettes of small, overlapping leaves also help conserve moisture. Rainfall may drain away very quickly on rocky mountains and plants can dry out quickly in strong winds. The white limey secretion on the leaves of this plant is thought to help reflect strong sunlight.

NATIVE PLANTS

The **ROCK GARDEN** displays plants from alpine and wetland regions of the world, grouped geographically. Part of the Rock Garden is devoted to British native plants including both rare and more common species, such as marsh marigold (*Caltha palustris,* below). We plan to store seed samples from every species of native plant in the Millennium Seed Bank, at Wakehurst Place.

HIGH

Alpines often have brightly coloured flowers making them a natural choice for gardeners (gentian, below). In the wild the bright colours are essential for attracting scarce pollinators during the very short growing season. Many species can also multiply by self pollination, or by growing runners or bulbils, in case there are too few insects.

S ome of the toughest plants are also some of the simplest. On the cold, barren lands near the north and south polar regions the most successful plants are tiny mosses and lichens, while some forms of red algae there are able to live on the surface of ice itself. Some small herbaceous plants and dwarf shrubs have also become adapted to withstand the high winds, lack of water (because plant roots can't absorb ice), freezing cold and poor soils. Similar conditions are found in high mountains such as the European Alps, North American Rockies, Asian Himalayas, African highlands and South American Andes. But here, too, plants survive thanks to some remarkable characteristics.

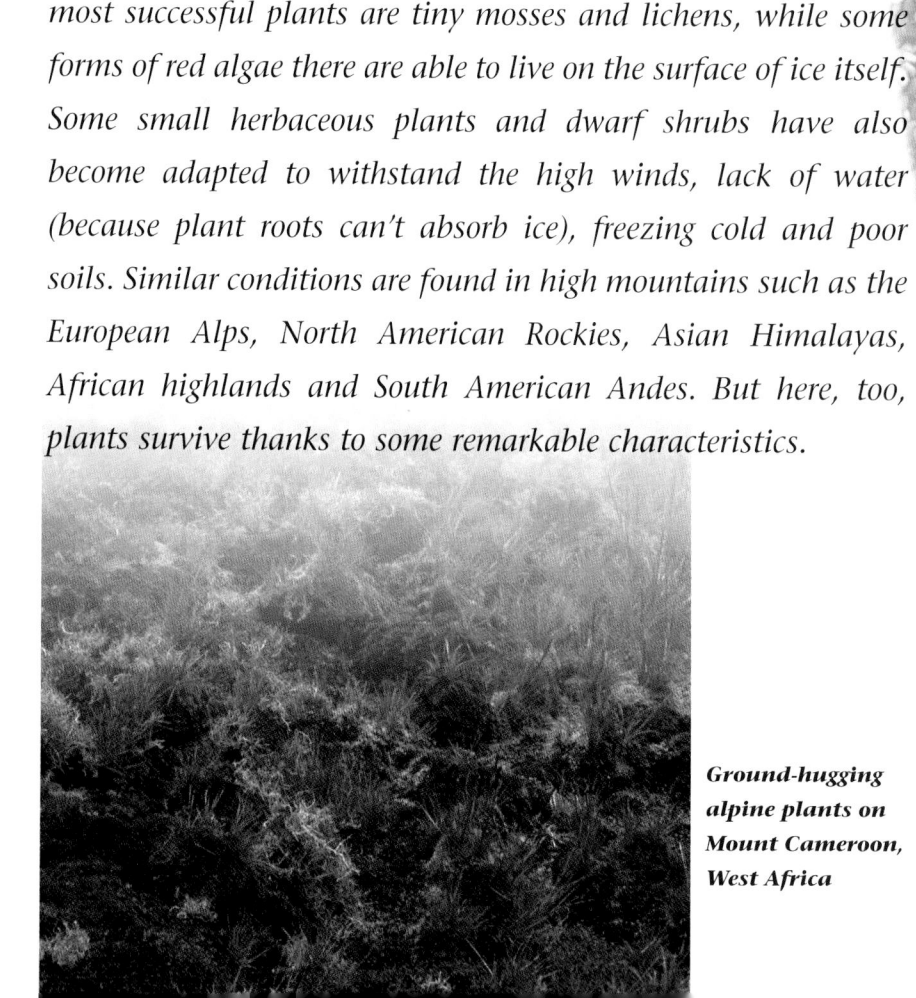

Ground-hugging alpine plants on Mount Cameroon, West Africa

The red pigment on the leaves of some alpines helps protect the green tissues against ultra-violet radiation (the rays that give people sunburn). The energy they absorb also helps keep the plant warm – up to twelve degrees warmer than the surrounding air (*Sempervivum tectorum*, above).

BEETLES ON THE SCENT

When Kew's Director, Sir Ghillean Prance, was working in the Amazon forests he discovered that the huge flowers of the giant Amazon waterlily are pollinated by beetles. The white flowers first open just before dusk. Their scent attracts beetles which make their way inside the flower, where they spend a cozy night feeding on nectar. During the night, the flower closes, and remains so until next evening, when it opens once again to let the beetles out. Just before it opens it releases its pollen onto the beetles. Off they fly, in time to get on the scent of the next batch of newly opening blooms. As they check in for the night, they brush against the female parts of the flower, thus helping the plant to cross-pollinate.

The most spectacular aquatic plant at Kew is the giant Amazon waterlily (*Victoria amazonica*) in the PRINCESS OF WALES CONSERVATORY. Its leaves can grow to almost three metres across and are supported by massive ribs that help resist tearing. Barbs on their lower surface discourage grazing by fish.

FLOATING LEAVES

Waterlilies come from one of the oldest lines of flowering plants and have spread through both tropical and temperate regions. They can be seen in the AQUATIC GARDEN, WATERLILY HOUSE and PRINCESS OF WALES CONSERVATORY. They grow in still water so can produce large round leaves on the surface. Leaves floating on water are easily damaged by raindrops because they do not 'give'- as leaves borne in the air can, so waterlily leaves have a strong waxy surface for protection.

Some freshwater plants are completely free-floating, kept buoyant with spongy, air-filled leaves or stems. Some of these plants, such as the water hyacinth you can see in the PRINCESS OF WALES CONSERVATORY pool, grow so fast that they are troublesome weeds. Chemical herbicides are difficult to use in water without killing other plants so some botanists are looking at ways of controlling these plants without using chemicals.

Waterlily leaf stalks must be capable of growing fast, to keep the leaves on the surface as the water rises after rain. Those of some waterlilies can grow up to 17 millimetres in one hour.

*F*resh water may be essential for plants but living in lakes and rivers presents its own challenges. In flowing water, plants run the risk of being damaged or even torn away by the flow so have evolved streamlined leaves and stalks which bend in the current.

PLANTS Ⓚ

HOLDING FAST AGAINST THE FLOOD

Kew botanists are studying plants that grow in narrow tropical mountain valleys and on riverbanks downstream, where flash floods are frequent. Although these plants do not spend all their time in flowing water they do have to withstand very strong currents during these floods. Although they come from a number of different and unrelated plant families they show remarkably similar adaptations to help them survive. They have strong root systems; very supple stems that bend easily without snapping; their leaves are often long and narrow, offering little resistance to water currents. Many of them have protective clusters of leaves around the flower buds. The picture shows *Kanahia laniflora* from Africa, which can be seen in the TEMPERATE HOUSE.

Like those of our native willow, the flexible stems of many of these plants are used by local people for basketry and may possess other characters useful to people.

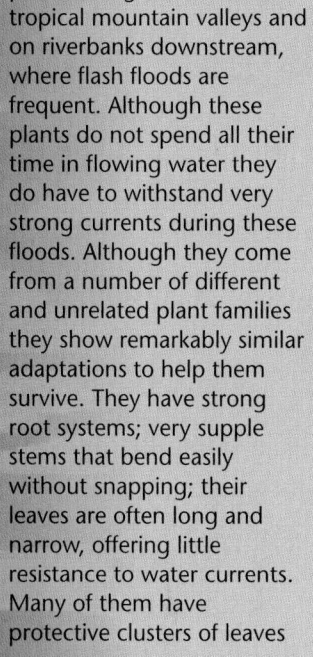

On the PALM HOUSE POND and the LAKE you can see many types of water-fowl, both visitors and residents. Those you are most likely to see include swans; shelduck; wigeon; gadwall; eider, mandarin, shoveler and tufted ducks; pochard; barnacle, greylag and pink-footed geese.

BETWEEN LAND & WATER

Marginal plants are those which live along the banks of lakes and rivers, or in marshy areas that are neither open water nor dry land. Irises and reedmaces can be seen in the AQUATIC GARDEN *and around the* LAKE *and ponds at Kew; tropical species such as papyrus, from which the Egyptians made their paper, are found in the* WATERLILY HOUSE *and the* PRINCESS OF WALES CONSERVATORY.

In the ROCK GARDEN *is a special boggy area where you can see species from the wetlands of Europe and North America.*

The roots of marginal plants are full of air spaces that link up to the stem so they can obtain air in waterlogged conditions. They are also very efficient in obtaining nutrients from the water and some have potential to clean water containing sewage and some types of industrial waste.

FRESHWATER

Life in lakes, ponds and tropical pools is less tranquil than it appears

MANGROVE SWAMPS

Only a few highly specialised plants live along tropical shores. Along many such shores are mangrove swamps. They are a particularly important habitat as they are the nursery grounds of many species of the fish and crustaceans on which local economies depend. They also offer excellent protection against hurricanes. For this reason many countries have now established mangrove replanting programmes but there are still some places where mangroves are endangered through drainage, building development and being cut for their wood.

Mangrove trees – such as *Rhizophora* and *Avicennia* species – can survive the twice-daily swamping by salty water and can gain a firm hold on the shifting mud. As you can see in the tanks in the **MARINE DISPLAY** and by the pool in the **PRINCESS OF WALES CONSERVATORY**, they have special 'snorkels' or pneumatophores which stick up through the mud to draw oxygen to the roots. Other types of root, called prop roots, support the trunks. Mangroves are able to remove the poisonous sea-salt from the water that enters the roots.

Mangrove seeds germinate before they fall and either float off to start a new colony or become firmly embedded in the mud between tides.

CORAL REEFS

Coral reefs are built by tiny animals related to sea anemones. Many have algae living in their tissues and these are the types which secrete minerals to build the reef's skeleton. Coral reefs are an important habitat, not just for plants but because they provide shelter for a fantastic diversity of tropical fish, some of which are important as food for humans.

The reef shelters its lagoon from the waves of the open ocean and much larger algae can gain a hold on the sandy sea floor. Caulerpa, one of these algae, is remarkable because – unlike the majority of large plants – it is not made up of a vast number of cells doing different jobs. Caulerpa is just one huge tube-shaped cell, yet can grow 'roots' down to gain a foothold into the sand or 'leaves' to absorb light and oxygen from the water.

SALT-MARSH

Like the mangroves, the plants of Britain's salt-marshes must be able to cope with shifting mud and daily flooding with sea-water. The glasswort *(Salicornia),* has a particularly unusual way of helping its seedlings to survive.

The seeds germinate while still attached to the already firmly-anchored parent plant, but as they germinate the parent dies. The seedlings root through the dead parent's roots, so are protected from being washed away by the tides. Salt-marsh plants are an important means of protecting low-lying land from erosion by the sea and can be planted as a form of coastal defence.

Visiting a Kew Gardens that truly reflected the importance of water plants to the world would be an uncomfortable experience. Two thirds of the gardens would be flooded and instead of a quiet stroll past beautiful flowers you would be in a wet-suit, admiring tiny algae through a microscope.

Life on Earth began in water, with ancestors of the single-celled algae that live in seas, lakes and rivers today. In total, these abundant plants produce more of the oxygen we breathe than any other plants – more, even, than the combined output of the giant trees of tropical rainforests.

At Kew you can find a taste of the diversity of aquatic plant life, from elegant waterlilies to the beautiful marine algae of tropical coral reefs.

ROCKY SHORES

Rocky shores are one of the harshest environments on Earth. Waves crash against rocks with immense force; when the tide goes out plants living on the rock face are exposed to baking sun in summer or bitter cold in winter – and they can dry out completely between tides. Seaweeds produce a slippery lubricating slime to prevent damage as they slide over rocks and to help the plant conserve water between tides.

BEHIND THE MARINE DISPLAY

Maintaining the algae in Kew's Marine Display is one of the more complicated tasks in the Gardens. Seawater is a complex mixture of chemical and biological ingredients which has to be kept clean and in the correct balance. Light and nutrient levels mimic those found in nature. Violent currents and tides must be provided for the rocky shore plants to survive. Coral reefs need water above 20 degrees Celsius, while bladderwracks can only survive below 13 degrees.

Marine algae are the most abundant of all plants. The Marine Display shows four of the most important marine ecosystems.

SEAWATER PLANTS

CONSERVING RAINFORESTS

We are working closely with colleagues in Limbe Botanic Gardens in West Africa, to help conserve the rainforests of Mount Cameroon. These forests, home to many unique species of plants and animals, are one of the top 20 conservation priorities in the world. The Friends of Kew has raised funds for botanical research in these forests and for projects that help local people make use of forest products while conserving the habitat.

THE CANOPY

The tallest rainforest trees can reach 70 metres and their heads thrust above the forest canopy for light. They have very straight trunks with buttress or stilt roots for support. The canopy of tall trees shields plants lower down against heavy tropical storms – the leaves filter the raindrops, breaking them up into a fine mist. Birds of prey patrol the canopy looking for a meal.

The **PALM HOUSE** gives you just a taste of what it is like to walk through a real rainforest. Once you have adapted to rainforest-style heat and humidity, one of the first things you notice is that different species of plants grow to different heights so that all the available space is taken up. It is the intense competition for space, light and nutrients that has driven the evolution of so many species.

THE MIDDLE LAYER

Layers of smaller trees grow beneath the protective canopy, the tallest of these may reach almost the same height as Kew's Pagoda, 50 metres. Climbers scramble through and among them while epiphytic plants grow on their branches – drawing moisture not from the soil way below but directly from the humid atmosphere or from rivulets running down the tree trunks. There is little wind here, so plants depend on insects, birds or bats for pollination. They may have highly scented or brightly coloured flowers to attract attention. Tasty, brightly coloured fruits encourage animals to eat them, to disperse the seeds.

THE FOREST FLOOR

The forest floor is too dark for most plants. It is covered by a dense layer of decaying leaves and here tree seedlings may wait in suspended animation, until an older tree dies and falls to leave space for the next generation. Some plants which grow at ground level have large thin leaves to absorb as much light as possible. Some, such as African violet, have become popular houseplants because they are so good at surviving in dim light.

At Kew we are learning more and more about the amazing diversity of rainforest plants. Some of the fruits of this work can be seen in the PALM HOUSE and PRINCESS OF WALES CONSERVATORY.

A single hectare of woodland in southern England is likely to contain about 10 or 15 species of flowering plants. In the same area of rainforest you could easily find 300. It is this diversity that makes rainforest conservation so important.

Rainforests are found in a broad belt to the north and south of the equator. The largest areas are in the Amazon basin in South America, the Congo basin of Africa and in South-East Asia. We undertake research and conservation in each of these areas.

The warm equatorial temperatures and high rainfall are ideal for plant growth. Rainforest soils often do not retain many plant nutrients and the plants which grow there have evolved to make the best use of what is available. If such forests are cleared for agriculture they can often support crops for only a few years before the soil is exhausted.

RAINFOREST
Tropical forests are home to the world's greatest diversity of plants

EPIPHYTES

A big challenge for plants growing in dense tropical forests is obtaining enough light. Trees have massive trunks to carry their light-gathering leaves high up. Other plants hitch a free ride on them. These 'epiphytes' (below) obtain the light they need by growing high up in the branches of trees.
They are too far from the ground to obtain moisture from the soil so they absorb it from the air or collected rainwater. In the PRINCESS OF WALES CONSERVATORY you can see ferns such as the birds nest fern (*Asplenium* species) or stags horn fern (*Platycerium* species), which obtain moisture from rainwater trickling down the tree trunks on which they grow. Nutrients are absorbed from fallen leaves trapped by their fronds. You can also find many species of bromeliads. Their rosettes of leaves look like pineapples and trap moisture at their base – habitats for insects and even small frogs.

The peaceful **FILMY FERN HOUSE**, behind the Orangery, with its collection of moisture loving sub-tropical and temperate ferns

ORCHIDS

The orchids are the largest family of flowering plants, with some 25,000 known species. Yet they are also one of the most recent families to have evolved. Evolution within the orchid family has resulted in a tremendous variety of flower shape and size and some amazing mechanisms for attracting pollinators and ensuring cross-fertilisation. Bee orchids, for example, imitate the appearance and scent of a female bee to attract male bee pollinators. The Madagascan orchid, Angraecum sesquipedale, *can only be pollinated by a single species of hawkmoth with a very long tongue. Botanists still do not fully understand the mechanisms that drive the evolution of such close relationships. Kew's orchid collection contains about 5,000 species, some of them can be seen in the* PRINCESS OF WALES CONSERVATORY. *Two different climate zones house orchids from the tropical lowlands and from tropical highlands or temperate regions. About 80 per cent of orchid species grow in the branches of tropical forest trees, often absorbing moisture direct from the humid atmosphere. Others grow on the ground or scramble over rocks – such as* Paphiopedilum insigne, *which has spread among rock crevices in the Conservatory much as it would do in its native India. Temperate orchid species can be found in the* ALPINE HOUSE, *the wetland area of the* ROCK GARDEN, *and the* WOODLAND GARDEN.

HUMID PLACES

H

I*n warm, humid, frost-free regions of the tropics and sub-tropics, plants can grow all year round. The greatest variety of plants is found in these parts of the world, which is why they are a focus of attention for Kew's botanists. Hundreds of plant species new to science are still being discovered every year.*

Plants from these regions can be found in the three great conservatories at Kew: **PRINCESS OF WALES CONSERVATORY,** *the* **PALM HOUSE** *and the* **TEMPERATE HOUSE.**

The five different environmental zones of the PRINCESS OF WALES CONSERVATORY *that house plants from moist tropical environments have sophisticated computer controlled heating, humidity, lighting and ventilation systems to provide ideal conditions.*

ISLAND PLANTS

Islands have more than their share of rare species. Few seeds reach them and those that do have few competitors. Over the generations new species evolve to fill empty habitats and each island ends up with its own set of unique plants. On tiny islands, human impacts make these botanical oddities vulnerable to extinction.

Kew is helping bring the most endangered island plants back from the brink. For example, one project of the Kew Island Plants Programme is on the Indian Ocean island of Rodrigues, where we are helping to restore woodland and conserve the beautiful but endangered *Hibiscus liliflorus*.

Only two plants still survive in the wild but we have located specimens in botanic gardens around the world and established a propagation programme on the island to produce seedlings. Look out for island rarities in the conservatories, and for the amazing flora of the Canary Islands in the **PRINCESS OF WALES CONSERVATORY.**

CARNIVORES

Carnivorous plants have always held a peculiar fascination. They obtain their energy from the sun, like all green plants, but they need 'meat' to obtain traces of nutrients such as nitrogen and some minerals. They grow on boggy soils where these nutrients are scarce.

In the Carnivorous Plant Display in the **PRINCESS OF WALES CONSERVATORY** you can see the range of methods which these plants use to trap and digest insects.

Venus fly-trap (*Dionaea muscipula*, top left) traps insects within specialised leaves which close when the insect lands on them. The

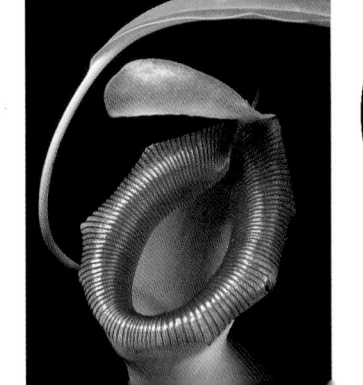

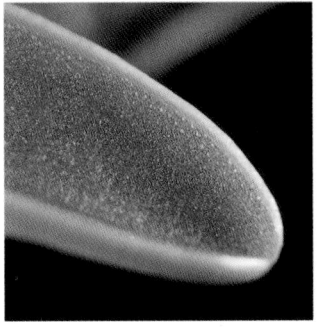

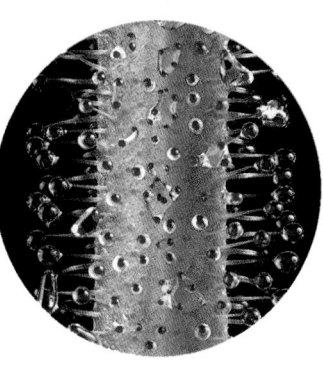

butterworts (*Pinguicula* species, top right) have flat leaves covered in sticky glue. Pitcher plants (*Nepenthes* species, bottom left, and *Sarracenia*) lure insects by smell and colour into their pitfall traps. Sundews (*Drosera* species, bottom right) have tentacles which wrap around the insect.

Many carnivorous plants' habitats are being drained and cleared for agriculture or building and plants are collected from the wild to supply the 'enthusiast' trade.

Droseras and pinguiculas can also be seen in the **ALPINE HOUSE**; North American pitcher plants (*Sarracenia*) can be seen on the wetland area of the **ROCK GARDEN.**

In the PRINCESS OF WALES CONSERVATORY *are 10 different environmental zones, each controlled by sophisticated computerised heating, humidity, lighting and ventilation systems to provide ideal conditions for plants from tropical habitats ranging from dry deserts to lush, humid cloud forests.*

The succulent leaves of Lithops, or stone-plants, are adapted in two ways to life in dry conditions. They act as a reservoir, storing water from mist and occasional rain; and they resemble stones, so are overlooked by grazing animals in a land where there are few plants for them to eat.

USING DESERT PLANTS

Brazil's semi-arid north-eastern region is one of the world's centres of plant diversity. Yet the people who live there use only a fraction of this botanical wealth, with traditional farming methods that can no longer meet the demand for food, fuel and building materials.

Since 1991 we have been involved in a series of projects known as Plantas do Nordeste, in which we work with Brazilian colleagues to identify plants native to North-East Brazil which could be better used by local people.

Already we have identified medicinal plant species which can be grown in living pharmacies next to local hospitals, to provide readily available, cheap, safe remedies. And we have helped develop a way of grazing goats and sheep on the scrubby vegetation which not only increases milk yields but allows the plants to grow back, avoiding the risk of overgrazing turning the land to desert. Areas where animals are grazed are divided into three sections, allowing a form of 'crop rotation', and the farmers are shown how to manage the vegetation to increase forage production and obtain multiple uses from the trees.

DESERT PLANTS

Fans of Western movies know the familiar features of the cacti – the archetypal desert plants. But as you can see in the PRINCESS OF WALES CONSERVATORY there are many other plant families with members adapted to desert conditions. For example, in Africa many species of the unrelated euphorbia family have adapted to desert life, and have evolved similar features to cacti: swollen stems to store water, waxy 'skins' to slow evaporation and prickles to protect themselves from grazing animals.

There are other ways for plants to survive in a desert. About half of all desert species spend most of their lives as drought-resistant seeds; or below ground as a dormant bulb, tuber or rhizome. In some regions there may be a rainy season once a year, in others it may only rain once every few years – but when it does these plants burst into brief, bright life. In as few as 30 days they grow leaves and produce flowers, set seed and die. Those with underground storage organs will have replenished their reserves ready for the next rains; others put their all into their seeds, relying on the next generation for the species' survival.

Perennial plants such as cacti and scrubby trees such as mesquite have extensive root systems. The mesquite's can be up to 53 metres long while cacti have a fine network of roots near the surface to absorb moisture after rain or heavy dew. In deserts close to the sea, such as the Namib in South-West Africa, cold fogs roll in from the sea and plants absorb moisture direct from the air. The most spectacular is *Welwitschia mirabilis* (left) whose two long leaves can be scores of years old.

As there is so little to eat in semi-arid regions, the plants that grow there must protect themselves from the attentions of grazing animals. Cacti, and many types of desert shrubs, are armed with defensive spines and prickles. Some plants, such as acacias, produce nectar to feed colonies of ants which live on them. The ants, which have painful stings, repel grazing animals. Other plants produce chemical toxins as animal repellents, some of which have been used medicinally.

ARID LANDS

lmost one in six of the world's people live on the edges of
deserts. Conditions are harsh and unpredictable. Droughts,
sometimes coupled with inappropriate farming techniques,
can lead to the spread of deserts. Increasing areas of land in
Asia, Africa and South America can no longer support
humans, nor the specialised communities of plants and
animals that have evolved to live in the desert margins.
These so-called semi-arid lands have become one of the
world's most threatened and fragile ecosystems. Many of
Kew's research projects are aimed at discovering more about
the plants that live there. Our botanists are finding species
adapted to semi-arid lands that can be planted or sustainably harvested to meet human needs for food, fuel and fodder for animals – and perhaps help halt the spread of deserts.

FIBRES

The Panama hat plant (*Carludovica palmata*) can be seen in the **PALM HOUSE**. Although it has palm-like leaves it is not, in fact, a palm. The young leaves are collected, washed and dried, bleached and plaited to make the hats. The fibres are extremely flexible so the hat regains its shape even after being rolled or squashed. There are many fibre producing plants at Kew, perhaps the most surprising being pineapple – fibres from the leaves are used to make cloth.

GRASSES AND BAMBOOS

The grass and bamboo family (known botanically as the Gramineae) is one of the largest families of flowering plants and is certainly the most important to humans. The family includes the cereal crops such as rice, wheat, maize, barley and millet. Rice (Oryza sativa) alone feeds more than half the human race. It thrives in waterlogged soil in the flood-plains of major Asian rivers such as the Ganges and Mekong.

Sugar cane (Saccharum officinarum) is also a grass. It originated in New Guinea but sugar has been produced from cane since 3,000BC in India. Now 66 million tonnes are produced around the world each year. In Brazil the alcohol by-product of cane sugar refining has been used to fuel cars – it is cleaner than oil and a renewable source of energy.

Bamboos are perhaps the most spectacular members of the grass family. They provide many of the materials for everyday life throughout the Far East and were cultivated in China more than 2,000 years BC. The young shoots are eaten and the canes are used to make products as diverse as boats, furniture, musical instruments, paper and even scaffolding, as seen here.

Cereals can be seen in the GRASS GARDEN *and* TEMPERATE HOUSE; *rice in the* PRINCESS OF WALES CONSERVATORY *and* WATERLILY HOUSE; *bamboos in the* BAMBOO GARDEN, PALM HOUSE, TEMPERATE HOUSE *and* SECLUDED GARDEN.

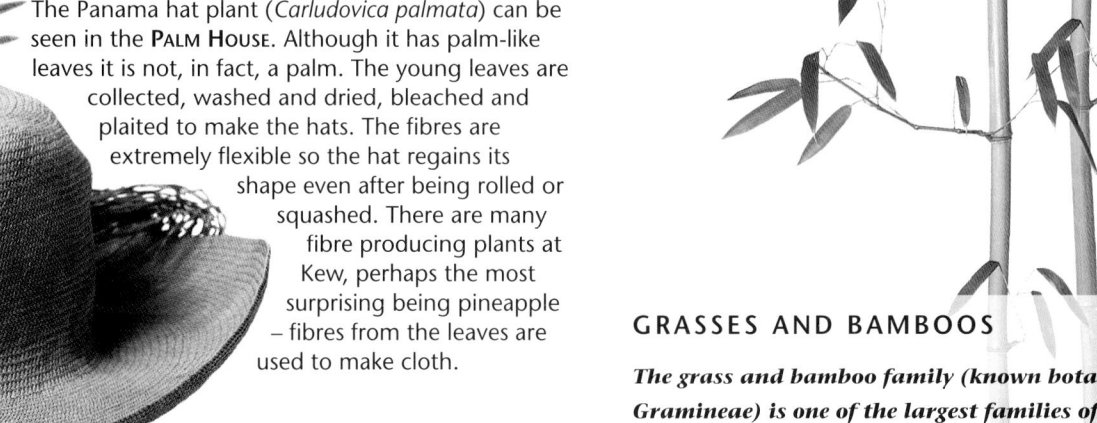

USEFUL PLANTS

F

K ew Gardens has a long history of research-ing the potential uses of plants. Kew's first, though 'unofficial' director, Sir Joseph Banks, sent plant collectors around the world looking for unusual species to send back to Kew. He believed one of Kew's roles was to seek plants which could have strategic or economic importance so he instructed his collectors to note any local uses for the plants they found. Sir William Hooker, Director from 1841 to 1865, established the Museum of Economic Botany to show how different peoples around the world made use of the plants they found growing around them.

RUBBER AND OTHER PRODUCTS

Rubber trees (*Hevea brasiliensis*) have a long association with Kew. In 1876 Kew received 70,000 rubber tree seeds, collected from Amazonian Brazil. They were planted here and some of the seedlings were sent to Sri Lanka and Malaysia where they became the basis for the huge Asian rubber plantations. Rubber is made from the white latex which flows from the inner bark of the tree when a series of cuts is made into the bark. It has qualities impossible to reproduce in synthetic material and more than 50,000 different products depend on it. Rubber tapping is still an important source of income for people living in the forests of Amazonia.

Rubber trees can be seen in the **PALM HOUSE**. Look out, too for papyrus (**WATERLILY HOUSE**) used by the ancient Egyptians for paper-making; the rice paper plant (**TEMPERATE HOUSE**), ebony (**PALM HOUSE**), jojoba (**TEMPERATE HOUSE**) used as an oil in cosmetics and the loofah (**WATERLILY HOUSE**), a relative of the familiar cucumber.

MEDICINES

The bitter drug quinine is the original, and still widely used, treatment for malaria, a tropical disease spread by mosquitoes. It comes from the bark of species of *Cinchona,* a South American evergreen plant. The drug was brought to Europe in the 1600s but by the early 1800s wild trees had been recklessly exploited, making quinine prohibitively expensive. Expeditions to South America, including some by Kew, collected seeds and plants which were used to start *Cinchona* plantations in India and the Far East, where malaria was rife. *Cinchona* bushes can be seen in the **TEMPERATE HOUSE**. Other plants with medicinal uses at Kew include *Brugmansia* and *Eucalyptus* species in the **TEMPERATE HOUSE** and Madagascan periwinkle, the source of two drugs used to treat leukaemia, in the **PALM HOUSE**.

Evans
250
Quinine Bisulphate
Tablets BP 300 mg
Sugar coated

Evans Medical Ltd.
Greenford, Middlesex

FLAVOURINGS

Vanilla, made from the seed pods of an orchid (*Vanilla planifolia*), is one of the most important flavourings in the world, earning significant income for Madagascar and several smaller islands in the Indian Ocean. It originates from Central America, where it was used by the Aztecs to flavour cocoa. The pods have to be fermented for a long period to release the vanilla flavour, a costly, labour intensive process.

You can see vanilla vines in the PRINCESS OF WALES CONSERVATORY and the PALM HOUSE. Other important plant flavourings growing at Kew include pepper, allspice and tamarind in the PALM HOUSE and capers, a taste of the Mediterranean, in the TEMPERATE HOUSE.

PALMS

Palms can provide all the basic necessities of human life, from food and timber to medicine and writing materials. Commercially important products, from palms that can be seen in the TEMPERATE HOUSE, PALM HOUSE and PRINCESS OF WALES CONSERVATORY at Kew, include palm oil, coir fibre (used for matting and to produce peat-free garden compost), carnauba wax, rattans and sago. But because palms are so useful, some species are close to extinction in the wild.

We are currently undertaking research into a number of different types of palm, including the rattans, which grow as climbers. As well as discovering more about how palms evolved, we are finding new uses for them and discovering methods of sustainably harvesting palm products. This may provide an income for people living in areas where palms grow and provide an incentive for protecting natural populations.

Look out for the Chilean wine palm (ours is the world's tallest indoor plant) and date palm in the TEMPERATE HOUSE; rattans, oil palm and coconut palm in the PALM HOUSE. In the PRINCESS OF WALES CONSERVATORY pool is Ravenea musicalis, the only palm which starts its life under water. It was discovered in 1994 by a Kew botanist in Madagascar, where a remarkable diversity of palm species can be found.

USEFUL PLANTS

Plants are the ultimate source of all foods and many of the materials we use for everyday life. Some, such as the grasses, have come to play a particularly important role. But we use only a comparatively small number of the world's 250,000 species of flowering plants.

Kew's scientists investigate potential uses of plants – as sources of new medicines, fuels or fodder crops. Ethnobotanists work with indigenous peoples overseas to learn uses of plants which may be threatened with extinction. This kind of work is undertaken in partnership with collaborating institutions in the countries where the plants are found and any proceeds that result from the research can be shared to fund work such as plant conservation there.

EDIBLE FRUITS

Olive trees *(Olea europaea)* take so long to grow and yield fruit that many believe olive cultivation led to the development of stable civilisation around the Mediterranean – a farmer would plant olives not for himself but for his grandchildren. Unripe green olives, as well as ripe black ones, are picked to eat but both are inedible until they have been fermented in salt to remove the bitter flavour. As well as being eaten directly, olives provide olive oil – the basis of much Mediterranean cooking as well as a source of oil for lamps. The oil is pressed out of the fruit, the finest oil coming from the first, cold pressing. The remaining pulp is then pressed again, sometimes using heat, producing poorer quality oil. Olives are related to ash trees, privet and lilac and can be seen in the TEMPERATE HOUSE. Look out, too, for citrus fruits (TEMPERATE HOUSE) and macadamia nut, mango and breadfruit (PALM HOUSE).

DRINKS

Cocoa *(Theobroma cacao)* can be seen growing in the **PALM HOUSE** where it occasionally bears its orange, rugby ball shaped pods, which contain the seeds or 'beans'. The Aztecs of Central America called cocoa the food of the gods and only those of great importance were allowed to drink it. They drank it as a bitter drink made from ground, roast cocoa beans, maize and chilli pepper. Today cocoa beans are sweated and fermented before being dried, shelled and roasted to be made into cocoa or chocolate.

Look out, too, for coffee growing in the **PALM HOUSE** and tea in the **TEMPERATE HOUSE**. China root, used to flavour root-beer, also grows in the **TEMPERATE HOUSE**.

WHAT'S IN A NAME?

Every plant has a double-barrelled scientific name. The first part is the name of the genus, the second the name of the species. There are some 600 species of oak trees and all belong to the genus *Quercus*. The second name of the plant is its species name. The Turkey oak, *Quercus cerris,* is a fine tree but its timber splits on drying. The similar looking common oak, *Quercus robur,* yields timber suitable for a wide variety of uses. If you are looking for an oak to provide timber it clearly pays to be able to specify the right one. Oaks share some characteristics with beech trees, particularly in the structure of their tiny, wind-pollinated flowers. So oak and beech are grouped in the same family (Fagaceae) .

Blue, white and pink bluebells may look different but are all the same species. The plant, the Scots call bluebell is a quite different species, known as harebell in England.

Genetic fingerprint

Chromosome painting

THE ORDER BEDS

You can clearly see the resemblances between related species of the plant families represented in Kew's ORDER BEDS. Here, more than 3,000 species of herbaceous plants are arranged in family groups. Large families, such as the daisies, take up several beds. As well as seeing the resemblances between plants you can also see the amazing diversity to be found within the families. All members of the daisy family (Compositae), for example, share the same basic arrangement of tiny florets that make up the composite flower head (below).

But in the Order Beds there are species ranging from just a few millimetres to more than a metre tall. Elsewhere in Kew you can see Compositae species remarkably adapted for life in the bitter cold of high mountains or the burning heat of tropical deserts. The form of their leaves and stems varies enormously but their flowers are all remarkably similar.

EVOLUTION HOUSE

When we group plants into genera and families we try to use characteristics that reflect natural relationships. The similarities we notice in members of the daisy family are not just coincidence. According to the theory of evolution, dandelions and daisies look similar because they had a common ancestor in the prehistoric past, in the same way that humans and apes evolved from an ape-like animal now extinct. We recognise the evolutionary history of dandelions and daisies by placing them in the same family, the Compositae.

So when we study the relationships between species alive today we are also discovering something about how those plants evolved. And we can use clues from fossils of extinct species to help us sort out the relationships between today's plants.

Kew's EVOLUTION HOUSE, *near the* TEMPERATE HOUSE, *tells the 3,500 million year story of plant evolution. The story begins with a barren, lifeless world. The first true plants,* which first appeared over 600 million years ago, were ancestors of modern algae. Land plants first appeared 450 million years ago and the first vascular plants, together with ancestors of today's mosses and liverworts, soon evolved. A coal swamp dominates the House and shows the kind of vegetation that occurred 300 million years ago and formed the coal measures. Cycads appeared 200 million years ago, while the conifers and flowering plants, which dominate the world today, complete the story.*

Some species alive today, such as various mosses and horsetails, share many characteristics with ancestral types known only as fossils. These plants grow in the Evolution House representing ancestral types, along with remarkable models based on fossils, to show how plants were adapted to conditions in prehistoric times and to show how changing environmental conditions drive the evolution of the enormous diversity of plants Kew represents.

FAMILY TREES

D

M uch of what Kew's scientists discover about plants comes from asking a simple question – how are the estimated 303,000 species of plants (more than three quarters of which are flowering species) related to each other?

The way we classify plants, in groups that reflect their natural relationships – and name them to an international standard, so that the same name means the same plant from Kew to Kowloon – is the science of systematics. It means we can identify the many previously unknown plants we find every year and work out how they are related to those we already know. This is essential information for planning conservation, or searching for plants which may be useful to humans.

WHAT IS A SPECIES?

Plants are grouped according to the features they have in common. A species is the most basic group and all the members of a species have a unique combination of characteristics of leaf, stem, flower, fruit and seed. Often they are found in a particular geographical area and do not usually, in nature, breed with members of another species.

Species with some general characteristics in common are grouped into a genus, while several genera with some basic things in common are grouped into families, such as the grass family or daisy family.

TRACING EVOLUTION

Studying live plants from the Gardens, dried specimens in Kew's Herbarium, and analysing the plant's chemistry and genetics in Kew's Jodrell Laboratory, help us trace plant relationships.

Our scientists have pioneered techniques which use similarities in the chemicals produced by different species to reveal relationships between them. They can also read the information carried in the plant's genes – the chemical 'instruction books' that pass information about the plant's characteristics from the parent plants to their offspring.

The individual genes are arranged together – like books on a library shelf – along structures called chromosomes in the plant's cells. We have pioneered a way of treating the plant tissues to 'paint' the chromosomes with special dyes, which glow when illuminated under a microscope. Dyes that glow different colours can identify chromosomes from different species. If we believe a plant is a hybrid this technique can help us identify its parents.

We have also been taking 'genetic fingerprints' of plants. All plants have a copy of the genetic instructions for making chlorophyll, the green pigment which uses solar energy to produce sugar from carbon dioxide and water. But as the instructions have been copied down, through the countless generations of evolutionary time, 'typing errors' have crept in. The instructions still make sense and the chlorophyll still works – but by comparing these small differences between the genes in different species we can work out how closely related they are. The fewer differences, the more closely the species are related. Often the results confirm current thinking but they can also reveal some surprising and previously unknown relationships.

KEW'S DIVERSITY

PLANT MEDICINES

Salicylic acid, originally obtained from willow bark, is the active ingredient of the pain-killer, aspirin. This example of an early preparation of aspirin is held in our Economic Botany Collections

PRESERVED SPECIMENS

Our Herbarium houses a collection of more than seven million preserved plant and fungi specimens used by botanists in research and as an aid to plant identification. This is Salix alba, the white willow

WOOD STRUCTURE

The wood anatomy collection in our Jodrell Laboratory holds some 76,000 glass slides of wood sections, such as these willow twigs, used in microscopic studies

Reference number · Plant family · SALICACEAE · Genus · Species this plant is a hybrid so the parent species are also shown · SALIX × CHRYSOCOMA (S. ALBA VAR VITELLINA × S. BABYLONICA) · GARDEN ORIGIN. · Geographical origin some labels also show economic uses, if any

The plants in the gardens at Kew and Wakehurst Place all belong to our Living Collection, a living library of plants from around the world. But each plant is also represented in many of our other collections, which are used to help our scientific and conservation work. Here we show how just one very familiar plant, the willow, features in these collections.

TIMBERS

Polished wood from **Salix caprea,** *the goat willow, from the timber collection held in our Economic Botany Centre*

PLANTS IN ART

Botanical painting of **Salix montana,** *one of the more than 10,000 items of botanical art held in our Library and Archives*

PLANT PRODUCTS

A cricket bat, made from **Salix alba** *var.* **caerulea** *(cricket bat willow) and a west-country fish-trap made from stems of* **Salix triandra,** *the Dutch willow, from our Economic Botany Collection*

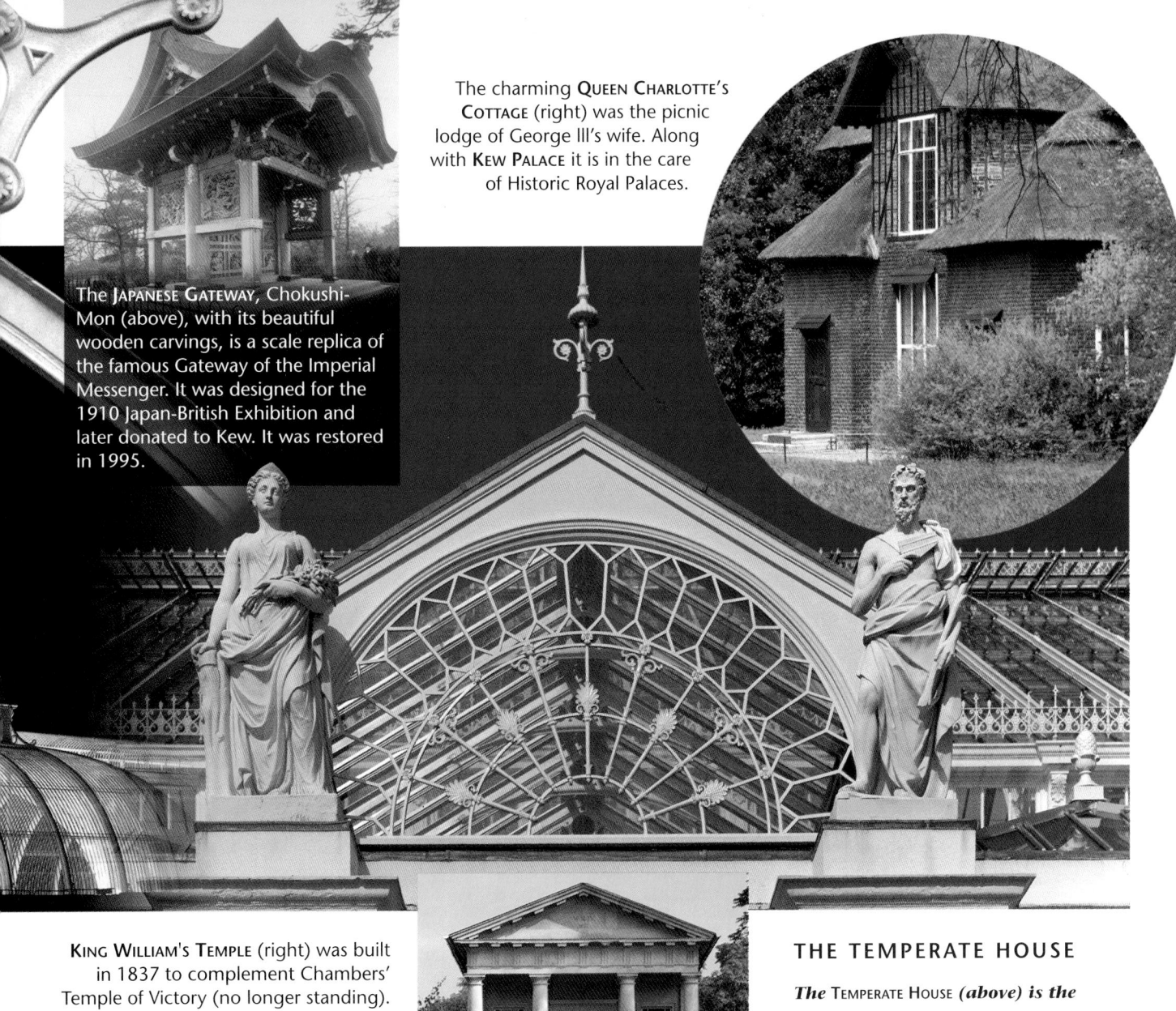

The charming **QUEEN CHARLOTTE'S COTTAGE** (right) was the picnic lodge of George lll's wife. Along with **KEW PALACE** it is in the care of Historic Royal Palaces.

The **JAPANESE GATEWAY**, Chokushi-Mon (above), with its beautiful wooden carvings, is a scale replica of the famous Gateway of the Imperial Messenger. It was designed for the 1910 Japan-British Exhibition and later donated to Kew. It was restored in 1995.

KING WILLIAM'S TEMPLE (right) was built in 1837 to complement Chambers' Temple of Victory (no longer standing). It was originally known as the Temple of Military Fame, and contains stone tablets recording British military victories from 1760 to 1815.

THE TEMPERATE HOUSE

The TEMPERATE HOUSE *(above) is the largest glasshouse at Kew (4880 square metres, twice the size of the Palm House) and was built in stages between 1860 and 1898, with a straight rather than curved profile to aid ventilation and, originally, wooden rather than iron glazing bars. The Temperate House was fully restored in the 1970s.*

The WATERLILY HOUSE *(right), with ironwork by Richard Turner, was built in 1852 for the giant Amazon waterlily. It was the widest single span glasshouse of its day – maximising the water area.*

The statue in the **GRASS GARDEN** is 'A Sower' (1886), by Sir Hamo Thorneycroft.

ARCHITECTURE Ⓑ

We have 39 listed buildings, including three of the world's greatest glasshouses

THE PRINCESS OF WALES CONSERVATORY

Energy efficiency was a key design feature of THE PRINCESS OF WALES CONSERVATORY *(right), completed in 1986. There are no side walls and much of the area is below ground level to conserve heat. The south-facing vertical walls make the most of winter light. Heating, lighting, ventilation and humidity are constantly adjusted by computer.*

The 10 storey, 50 metre tall **PAGODA** (below) was designed by Sir William Chambers for Princess Augusta and built in 1762 at a time when oriental-style garden buildings were popular.

Between 1757 and 1762, Chambers designed at least 25 buildings which were erected at Kew including a Mosque. Surviving designs include the **ORANGERY, RUINED ARCH** and **TEMPLE OF BELLONA** as well as the **PAGODA**.

THE PALM HOUSE

When the PALM HOUSE *(right) was built (1844-48) architect Decimus Burton insisted it was overlooking a lake so that it would be reflected in the water. It was Irish iron-founder Richard Turner who proposed using wrought iron 'deck beams' as used in ship-building to span the greatest possible width without internal pillars. The original glazing was green to shade the plants. The* CAMPANILE *near the* VICTORIA GATE *was a smokestack for the old* PALM HOUSE *heating boilers. The* PALM HOUSE *was extensively restored in the 1980s.*

The oldest building still standing in Kew Gardens is the Dutch-style **KEW PALACE**, built in 1631. Lovers of art and architecture can have just as fascinating a day at Kew as lovers of plants, following the changes in style from Chambers' classical buildings for the Royal garden through the Victorians' ornamented but purposeful glasshouses to the striking and ultra-modern Princess of Wales Conservatory. Kew's collections of botanical art are displayed in exhibitions in the **KEW GARDENS GALLERY** while the stunning paintings of Victorian traveller and artist Marianne North are housed in their own gallery.

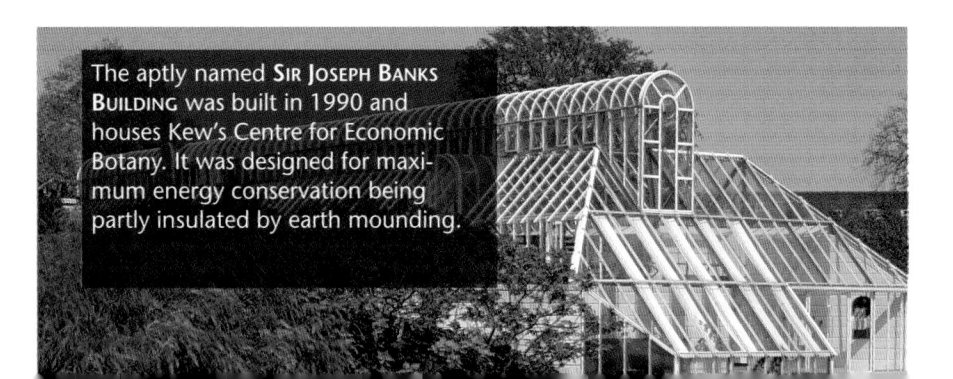

The aptly named **SIR JOSEPH BANKS BUILDING** was built in 1990 and houses Kew's Centre for Economic Botany. It was designed for maximum energy conservation being partly insulated by earth mounding.

1835

Plants reached Britain from Australia by ship, surviving the voyage in a sealed glass Wardian Case (named after inventor Nathaniel Ward). These cases played a key role in the transfer of living plants to and from Kew (rubber plants to Ceylon, *Cinchona* for quinine to India, tea from China) by providing ideal conditions for plants on long sea voyages. Kew used them until the 1960s.

1841

Following a period of decline after the death of George III and Joseph Banks (both in 1820), Kew was given to the nation. Sir William Hooker, the first Director, established Kew's scientific direction, with the Herbarium, Library and the Museum of Economic Botany to educate the public. The Palm House was built and the Temperate House started.

1865

Sir William's son, Joseph, took over the Directorship and continued work on the Temperate House. The Hookers, with Sir William Thistleton Dyer (Joseph's son-in law), mounted a robust and successful defence against politicians and others who wanted to dilute Kew's base as a scientific and educational institution and turn the Gardens into a pleasure park.

1896

Kew's first women gardeners were employed. They had to wear clothes 'unlikely to provoke male colleagues'. By 1917 there were more than 30 women gardeners, having replaced conscripted men fighting the First World War.

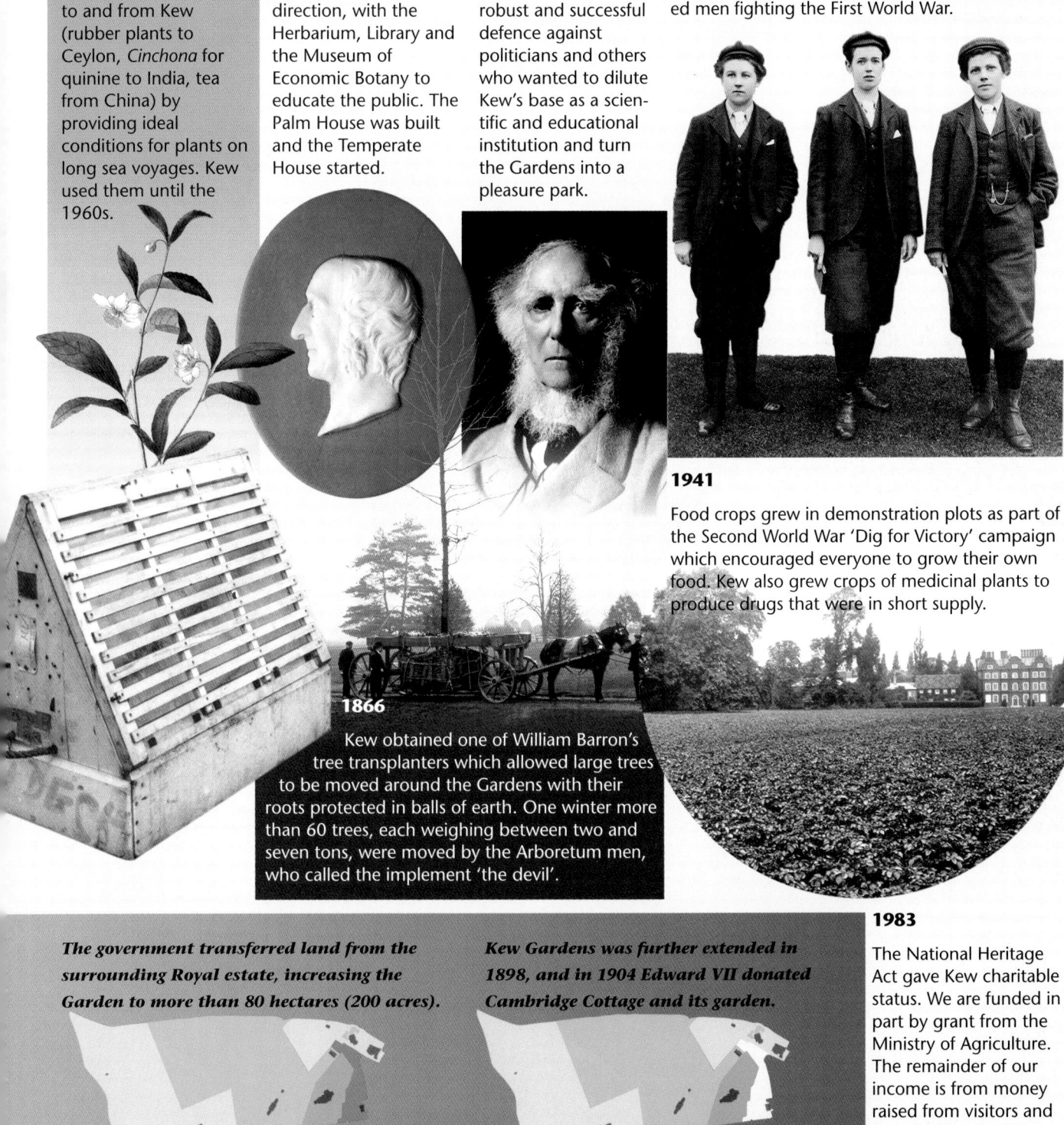

1941

Food crops grew in demonstration plots as part of the Second World War 'Dig for Victory' campaign which encouraged everyone to grow their own food. Kew also grew crops of medicinal plants to produce drugs that were in short supply.

1866

Kew obtained one of William Barron's tree transplanters which allowed large trees to be moved around the Gardens with their roots protected in balls of earth. One winter more than 60 trees, each weighing between two and seven tons, were moved by the Arboretum men, who called the implement 'the devil'.

The government transferred land from the surrounding Royal estate, increasing the Garden to more than 80 hectares (200 acres).

1841–45

Kew Gardens was further extended in 1898, and in 1904 Edward VII donated Cambridge Cottage and its garden.

1904

1983

The National Heritage Act gave Kew charitable status. We are funded in part by grant from the Ministry of Agriculture. The remainder of our income is from money raised from visitors and from funds raised from corporations and individuals by Kew's Foundation and Friends.

Ⓐ HISTORY

The Royal Botanic Gardens did indeed once belong to the Royal Family. The Hanoverian Prince and Princess of Wales lived here from 1718 and during the reign of George III the estate began to develop into a botanic garden of international importance.

1772

Sir Joseph Banks, wealthy landowner, entrepreneur, botanist and adventurer, met George III, owner of Kew. Banks had already accompanied Captain Cook on his voyage to discover Australia. Now he established himself as Kew's unofficial head, advising on its development and appointing plant collectors to travel the world in search of new plants. He organised the shipment of breadfruit plants from the Pacific island of Tahiti to the West Indies as a crop to feed slaves. Captain Bligh, master of *HMS Bounty*, was commissioned to do the job and two Kew gardeners found themselves on opposing sides in the notorious mutiny.

1755

The extraordinary Swan Boat, which used to float on the Lake, was made on the occasion of the Prince of Wales' (the future George III) birthday. Its neck and head reached 18 feet and it could carry 10 people.

1773

Strelitzia reginae was named by Banks in honour of George III's wife, the Duchess of Mecklenburg-Strelitz.

1750

Prince Frederick and Princess Augusta, the Prince and Princess of Wales, began to develop their estate at Kew with help from their friend the Earl of Bute, a competent plantsman who advised on landscaping, acquiring plants and recruiting staff.

When Augusta inherited Kew from her husband she implemented his plan to develop an exotic garden. Bute began to build up the botanical collections '...to contain all the plants known on Earth'. He also acted as tutor to the future George III, the next owner of Kew.

1784

William Aiton, who looked after the first botanical collections, became head gardener of the Kew estate.

The first botanical garden covered roughly the area between the present Orangery, Victoria Gate and Jodrell Laboratory.

George III inherited the Richmond and Kew estates. Part of the former boundary between them is marked by today's Holly Walk.

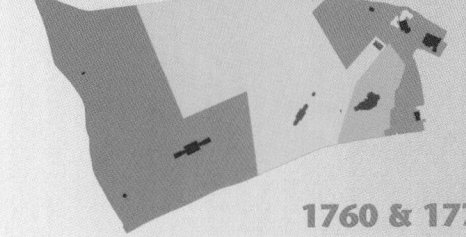

1759

1760 & 1772

The Many Faces of Kew

The Royal Botanic Gardens at Kew and Wakehurst Place are among the most beautiful gardens in the country. But their beauty is more than skin deep. Our collection of more than 40,000 different kinds of plants is the largest and most diverse collection of living plants in the world – one in eight of all flowering plant species grow here. But it is just one aspect of our world-wide plant research and conservation work. Kew also holds the world's most comprehensive collections of preserved plant specimens; plant products used by humans and botanical books, paintings drawings and literature.

CONTENTS

Section

INDEX

How to use this book

This book is more than just a guide to the Gardens. It can be used alongside your free Welcome to Kew leaflet to help you plan your visit and find your way around. But it also shows how the plants in the Gardens reflect our vital international conservation and research work and tells you more about our fascinating history.

The sections of the book reflect the main plant habitats represented at Kew, showing some of the plants and how our work is leading to a better understanding of them. We want you to share in our fascination for the Plant Kingdom and to find out more about what we do as well as what we are.

Use this map and the index on the left if you want to find the sections of the book which deal with particular parts of the Garden that interest you. Throughout the book, the locations where you can see the plants and habitats mentioned are highlighted in CAPITAL TYPE.